GW00372037

Lugworm Homeward Bound

To Bill,
who started it all

Lugworm Homeward Bound

**From Greece to England
in an Open Boat**

by

Ken Duxbury

Lodestar   Books

Lodestar Books
71 Boveney Road
London SE23 3NL
United Kingdom

www.lodestarbooks.com

First published 1975 by Pelham Books, London

This edition published by Lodestar Books 2012
Design copyright © Lodestar Books 2012

A catalogue record for this book
is available from the British Library

ISBN
978-1-907206-12-2 The Lugworm Chronicles (Trilogy)
978-1-907206-10-8 Lugworm Homeward Bound

Set in Adobe Garamond Pro
and **Nueva Bold Extended**

Printed in the UK by MPG Biddles, King's Lynn

CONTENTS

PLATES *(between pages 96 and 97)*

SKETCH MAPS

PREFACE

Corfu, April 1972

'*LUGWORM*' IS AN EIGHTEEN FOOT open sailing dinghy fitted with a four horsepower outboard motor, and she is the other heroine of this book. I had her built in 1969 for £485 and fortunately in the spring of 1971 went potty. It was *Lugworm*'s doing.

'B.,' I had said to my wife, who is mad enough too if caught at the right moment, 'let's pull out of business for good and tow the Drascombe Lugger overland to Greece. We'll potter around there this summer living aboard the boat and then sail her back to England next summer; it'll rout all the hysteria of the old life from our systems!'

So it had been arranged, though in honesty we couldn't afford it, which is why it is fortunate to be mad. The summer of 1971 has been spent fossicking about the Aegean and Ionian Seas getting used to sleeping aboard an open boat and learning to live again. Believe me, the two of us have got so bitten with a carefree nomadic existence that it seemed strange to settle for the winter in this house on the north of Corfu. But it has given me the opportunity to write a book on our Greek wanderings – and I hope very much you will buy it. It is called *Lugworm on the Loose* (Pelham Books) and costs £3.00 which is too expensive, but I haven't yet raised the courage for a row with my Publishers.

Now it is April 1972 and I'm writing this on the lawn looking across Corfu Strait to Albania six miles away. *Lugworm* is proudly bobbing at her anchor just off the white pebble beach below me – I can see the tops of her two small masts from here. She's packed with gear for the voyage and ready in all respects for sea. 'Foogoo', our hideous hand-carved African mascot, four inches of him, hangs by his obscene belly-button at the base of the mizzen mast, belligerently in charge – for have we not placed the responsibility for a successful voyage squarely in his hands? Since B. is in Kassiopi, the nearby village, shopping for the last bits and pieces, I can safely let you into a secret – I'm scared stiff!

Why? Hah! It's all very well in a potty moment to burble, 'We'll sail the dinghy back to England,' but I'll warrant if, like me, you were here and actually about to set off and do it – you wouldn't be seeing the first mark for butterflies either.

'What are you worried about?' I keep asking myself. 'It's only sixty miles across the Adriatic and then another two thousand six hundred or so more around the twiddly bits at the toe of Italy up through France; then, dammit, you're as good as home!'

Trouble is, I'm blessed with imagination – a bad fault in any sailor. I see roaring great breakers dashing our frail cockleshell against black cliffs. I see us skewered by swordfish, buffeted by whales; my dreams fill with oceans of wind-driven spume screaming across uncaring watery wastes, with B. and I clasped in each other's arms, gasping our last. Oh Hell!

No. I must get a grip and try to be responsible. It isn't ME I'm worried about, it's B. I've no right to risk her life like this, she's too young and beautiful. Of the thousand adventures that are going to arise in the next six months, one surely will be disastrous?

Duxbury you're a fraud! These butterflies have nothing to do with responsibility and noble thoughts, love or fear for B. You're just jellified.

So what? You've spent a lifetime at sea; you certainly know a darned sight more about seamanship and handling small boats than Noah and – Oh God! – look what he did!

OF COURSE it's a ridiculous thing to try to do in a dinghy. But if it comes off, won't it be GREAT talking and writing about it afterwards? Adventure – isn't that maybe what life's all about?

Um … Well …

But here comes B. round the bay with the last fresh milk we're going to see for many a month. And what's that she's carrying in her other hand?

Heaven above – it's an olive sprig!

I'm going to seal this page at the back of *Lugworm*'s log and alter not one word when – and if – we get home. Odd, but suddenly I've a firm conviction we shall.

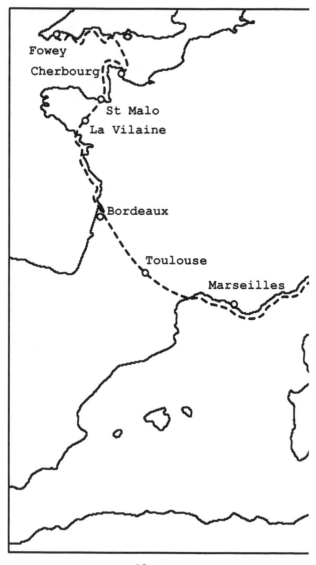

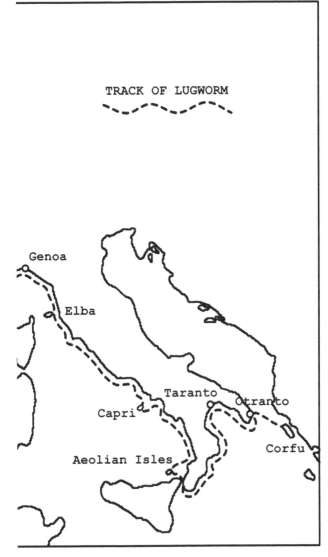

TRACK OF LUGWORM

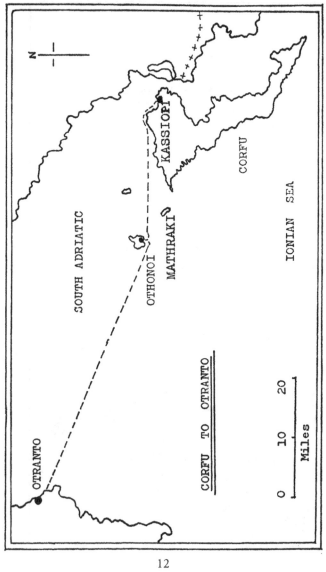

CHAPTER I

The Voyage Begins

GLANCE AT A CHART OF CORFU and you will see that there are three small islands off its north-western corner, the largest of which lies some twelve miles out into the Adriatic. Twelve miles, that is, nearer to Italy.

Now you may guess that the prime concern of anyone cruising in a small open boat is to avoid long open-water passages so much as may be possible. A yacht, fully decked and with ballasted keel, if overtaken by foul weather, is often well advised to stand off-shore into deep water and ride it out, but for a dinghy such as ours this could be fatal; she would too easily founder. So it is always wise to have some place of refuge ready to hand, preferably within an hour or so. Of course, this was going to be impossible on the crossing to Italy but it was common sense to make the crossing as short as we could.

That farthest island, called Othonoi, made a handy springboard for the leap, and you may be sure we had taken a few soundings locally. I remember one winter evening in the village taverna tackling our friend Christos about it over a glass of retzina. Christos is the Greek skipper of a fishing caique and a seaman down to his toenails, as well as being the only member of the village community who speaks any English.

'This island here,' I asked him, above the roar of the jukebox, spreading the chart over a table. 'It has a lighthouse but does anyone live there? The chart shows nothing. Is there any sort of harbour?' He elbowed his way across and pulled up a chair.

'You go here, eh? Yes, it is good but is vaary ... how you say ... leetle, eh? Few people there, a vaary leetle harbour and,' he shrugged and made that characteristic Greek gesture with his hands, 'for my boat no good. No water. A few feet maybe but ... how you say ... rifs ... rifts ... what you call those rocks under water?'

'Reefs.'

'That's it, exactly, exactly,' he agreed, using a phrase by which we'll always remember him. 'From a north wind it is good here. Here,' and he stabbed the chart with a gnarled forefinger. 'You anchor in this bay close to the harbour. But if the wind comes south – you get your boat ashore quick, eh?'

'What sort of beach?' chipped in B.

'Ammou Bay? All right there; for you good. Small stones, not steep. Your boat, you pull her up maybe, you ask, they will help, the people there.'

Which was comforting. We knew from experience that on the islands, and particularly where there were fishermen, we would never want for help. But it was a problem which was giving me concern for the voyage ahead. On those lonely stretches of coast along the instep of Italy there were few harbours and likely to be few people should sudden need arise. That, however, was a part of the challenge: a problem we would face when it came.

Meanwhile, on that sunny morning of the 19th April 1972, we were as prepared for the voyage as it is humanly possible to be, but – understandably I suppose – when it came to it, the sense of adventure and excitement was subdued by an unexpected sadness. As we walked for the last time across the rock strewn lawn, we glanced back at the house which had been our home for five very momentous months – and our eyes ranged on up the valley behind. It was a riot of yellow broom in the warm spring sunshine, crowned at its rim with silver-grey of the olive grove, and we knew and loved every bend, every ledge and crevass of that place. Our partings were over and done with in the village and now, at last, there was nothing for it but to bid 'adieu' to the house and valley and leave.

As we walked down to the boat, a sound – far away and hauntingly familiar – came floating from the hills and caused us to turn again. It was music which for us will ever bring with it the overpowering essence of Greece; elusive, hidden, seldom located but always there and half-heard – the voice of the very hills themselves, the distant trembling of goat bells.

'Ah,' said B., as she waded out to *Lugworm*, 'I'm not sure I like this much; I didn't think it would be quite so difficult, leaving it all; odd isn't it how you only find the real depth of the roots when you're pulling them up for ever!'

'Oh,' I said, 'we'll be back.'

'Maybe,' she answered, 'but it will never be quite the same again, will it?' And, looking at the raw wound of the great new highway scarring its way ever further along the shore and round behind the house, I knew what she meant. We looked back along the coast where the old fortress sprawled over the distant headland – you could see the bright flash of our secret beach where we found the cannon buried – and I saw B.'s eyes swing up the rocky skyline above the village to where the rugged shoulders of Pantokrator, Corfu's highest peak, towered under a cloak of white cloud. There far beyond and above the house was the familiar cypress tree, its green flame still burning the sky, and as we looked our attention was drawn to a small movement. Far up there a tiny figure stood dark against the grey rocks, but there was no mistaking that lean stance, nor the long roughspun cloak and hood; it was our friend Panayotis, the shepherd. Courteous, shy, always withdrawn, he had on rare occasions called at the house to replenish his flask of water and each time he brought some small gift with him, from the hills.

Impulsively we both stood and raised our arms in farewell. 'PANAYOTIS!' I shouted, 'PANAYOTIS ... YASSOU! GOODBYE!' In the complete stillness we listened to echoes reverberating up the sides of the valley, dying away in the hills above, and then incredibly – for he must have been nearly a mile away – we saw him face us and raise his staff in salute.

'Eyes and ears like a hawk,' I murmured, as I pulled in the anchor warp, and there was a long pause.

'Yes,' I heard B.'s soft answer, 'a strange people, so maddeningly unreliable, so infuriatingly naive, yet odd how they can make such a hole in one's armour.'

But *Lugworm* is stirring. Her three tan sails are feeling the first of the morning breeze and the near headland is approaching. It comes slowly up, drifts past, and now gently turns the page to conceal first the house, then the secret bay, then the village and the distant ruins; and last of all Panayotis still standing there in the hills, his staff held high like a benediction.

You must not be impatient. I know full well you want to learn all about *Lugworm*; how we slept in her, how we rigged the tent, stowed all the gear, cooked, dealt with storms, pulled her up the beaches, navigated, blew our noses and had rows aboard; and all will be revealed in good time. But if you're going to share the fun and excitement of this ridiculous adventure, dammit you're going to share the hardships too!

We might as well begin now. In case you don't know I'll tell you that it rains in Corfu in the winter. It rains with such ferocity and so continually that one might be forgiven for assuming it'll never stop. That is why the island is so green and thankful in the summer. April is when the rains finally relent and our moment of parting was one of those first bright smiles of spring.

It was no surprise to us however when, a couple of hours after rounding that first headland, we caught Pantokrator swapping his white cloak for an ominous dark grey shroud. We watched its shadow creeping down the near flanks of the hills to our south, spreading over the beaches and flat marshes of Saouli and Rodha, and already Mathraki island – southernmost of the three ahead – had turned into a black silhouette against the glowering sky. Othonoi, straight over our bow, was now an isolated shining green and white oasis. So calm had our day become, the island seemed supported by its own reflection in a liquid mirror. By noon we were not yet past the rocky Cape Dhrastis at the north-west tip of Corfu and were making no progress. What is more there were ominous rolls of thunder growling up there in the heights.

'I think we're for it,' I remarked to B. We well knew these jests of the weather; seldom did the rain come without a brisk frolic of wind out at sea, and if we were in for a squall, the closer we got to Othonoi before it arrived, the better. 'Best start the outboard and get all the loose gear stowed.'

An hour later we were both standing in oilskins as torrential sheets of icy water deluged from a black sky. When this sort of thing happens, it's far better to stand up because, apart from just not wanting to take it sitting down, you do then offer less actual surface to the slings and arrows. Our world, from being a place of bright warmth and colour, had shrunk to a cold grey circle; even the pale diluted ghost of the land was washed away as we puttered through a blanket of grey water with nothing but the compass to guide us. All about the sea was a spitting, hissing pewter plate, yet still, strangely, there was no breath of wind.

I'm not superstitious, but there are occasions when there's nothing to be lost by offering up a few verbal sacrifices. 'All powerful Poseidon,' I mumbled, peering miserably into the grey pall, for already I could feel that first clammy damp seeping through my oilskins between my shoulder blades, 'have mercy on us. You smiled and favoured us all last summer; have we offended in some way?' B. raised her eyebrows and started bailing. If possible, the torrent grew even fiercer. Then as sudden as the icy trickle that probed down my chest, came enlightenment. 'It's YOUR doing!' I bellowed at her above the roar of the rain. 'When were you born, eh? Pisces! The FISH!'

How clear it was! Discard Poseidon forthwith – was I not carrying in the very boat one of the Piscean shoal? Watery Pisces, so lately clutched to the bosom of planet Neptune; why it was plain as a cod's eye, to Neptune, Roman God of the sea I should shriek, not to Hellenic Poseidon whose domain we were in the very act of forsaking!

'All forgiving, beneficient, omniscient Neptune,' I roared, casting a cautious glance astern, 'Relent, for mercy's sake RE-LENT! We are but frail humans, lacking the gills to fully appreciate your aweful Kingdom!'

B. stopped bailing and looked at me in alarm. I saw her mouth working and caught, through the hiss of the deluge the words 'for better or for worse' and then – you won't believe me, will you, but that damnable rain fell away before a veil of blessed silence, and ahead, from out of the west, like a smile from the God himself, broke an avalanche of light. It swept aside the hideous dark clouds, bathing and nourishing our steaming forms in the warmth of that after-noon sunshine. And there, close aboard, were two leaping dolphins, leading us away from that awful pall. Oh! The blessing of that heat!

'You little waterwitch,' I admonished B. 'Why didn't you warn me? How can Foogoo and I hope to bring us safely through if the very Gods themselves sport with us?' She said not a word; indeed I believe she was too busy bailing even to hear, but as I pulled my sodden oilskin over my head, I swear I caught the glint of a scaly fish tail fast disappearing up one yellow trouser leg.

We sponged the decks, tossed out the final bucketful and mopped the bilges dry. Everything not actually battened in the lockers was sodden; even the chart which had been stowed in the netting tight up under the side-decks was pulpy with splashes and sagged limply on the bottomboards as we pored over it – for there, close ahead, was the island – and a quick bearing showed that our course would take us straight over the off-lying reefs. I brought *Lugworm* ten degrees to the south and together we scanned its shores.

Islands thrill me. Like humans, no one of them, wherever it may be, is quite the same as any other. It is unfortunate that the poverty of air travel, the isolation of the all-embracing cruise, can present their features as mere distressful repetitions, but this is due to the shallow perception such travel engenders: in fact every island has a flavour of its own, and the finest way to savour it is to approach slowly from afar in a small boat; to be embraced into its arms as a welcome traveller gaining shelter and hospitality.

Ahead of us in the bright sun, the thousand foot peak of Othonoi shone like a beacon, white on the waterline, green up the slopes, and broken with rugged grey outcrops in the higher parts. Already I could make out a straggle of houses, wavering and ridiculously tall in the mirage of the shore, while behind them two valleys probed back, dark with the shadow and translucent green of pine and cypress.

'There are boats in there,' said B., scanning the shoreline with the binoculars. 'I can see the masts; they look like small fishing craft.' As we surveyed the village, we saw that between us and the houses there occasionally appeared a small white line of breakers, and this riveted our attention. A kindly long swell, difficult to detect out here in deep water, was betraying the reefs.

'We'd better nose into the bay from due south,' I told her, 'then scout around and see how the harbour entrance lies.'

'Wait a minute,' she replied, still peering through the glasses. 'There's something coming through the reefs ... a small boat I think.'

Sure enough, dipping one moment completely out of sight, perched the next on the crest of a swell, a tiny rowing boat was working its way out between the breakers. As it approached we could see the figure of a small boy, rowing fiercely, glancing occasionally over his shoulder. When within hailing distance he shipped his oars and stood up, cupping his hands. We heard the call, *'Edho ... edho ...* (here ... here). Follow me!'

I unshipped our rudder from its trunking, hauled the metal centreplate right up, and B. hastily dropped the now dry sails to allow a clear view ahead. Steering with the outboard motor we nosed our way in behind him, and that boy certainly knew his channel. We passed within feet of the underwater rocks, now north, now east, now north again, creeping along and between the lines of white, following the grinning face of that imp, who couldn't have been more than ten years old at most, as he threaded us towards a tiny shallow harbour protected only by a low stone mole.

A group had gathered on a low concrete quay, and the boy indicated that we make fast there. But a long low surge, residue of the swell which crept through the reefs, would have caused

Lugworm to scrape her golden teak gunwales against the rough edge, which set me searching around for a kinder billet. This is one great advantage of our dinghy: she can float in ten inches of water, and often this fact has secured for us a birth of far greater comfort and privacy than was available to her larger sisters. Eventually we settled stem-to in a depth of eighteen inches with a bow anchor firmly lodged over an exposed rock, and a couple of stern-warps out on either quarter to hold her safe.

It was while I was eyeing the bottom to see that she was clear of any sharp projections that we first caught sight of the captive crabs – tied by strings and crawling about on the seabed all around us for all the world like pets on a lead. But of course this was just the islanders' sensible way of keeping them fresh for when they were needed in the pot. Some of them were huge, and B. viewed the whole situation with some misgiving but as I pointed out to her, 'They're quite harmless unless they bite you.' Which didn't help much.

It was gone 5 p.m. before all was secure. We thanked the child for his pilotage and did our best to satisfy the curiosity of the villagers who were intrigued by our boat, for though neither of us speak Greek fluently, we had by that time enough command of the everyday phrases to make ourselves partly understood.

'And now,' I said to B., casting a weather eye skyward, 'before we do anything else we'd better turn *Lugworm* into a Christmas pudding.'

In case you think me finally off my rocker, I had better explain that this is the term we use for rigging the tent, and indeed perhaps now I should introduce you more fully to this versatile craft of ours.

Lugworm is built of marine plywood, partly decked fore and aft, and with side-decks running down the length of the eight-foot open cockpit. This decking is overlaid with fibreglass matting bonded to the ply, a fact which has caused many people to think the boat is built wholly of this material. You may ask why just this part of the boat should be so treated, as I did myself when first seeing a Drascombe Lugger, and the answer is because her designer, John Watkinson, is a seaman who has cruised in small boats and knows a thing or two about life aboard. He knows, for instance, that the average dinghy sailor, when forced to cook on board, inevitably stands boiling saucepans on deck, spills burning methylated spirit over them, allows candles to burn out thereon and stabs them with sharp anchor flukes; generally misusing them in a way which rapidly reduces any varnished or painted surface to an unsightly mess. A hard armour-plating of fibreglass is virtually immune to all these evils, and I can say as I write this that *Lugworm*'s decks, after four thousand miles of cruising and over a period of some three seasons' hard use, remain almost as unblemished as the day we bought her.

She has two pine masts, the after of which – the mizzen – is unstayed and relies for its support on being fed down into a hole abaft the rudder slot, so that its toe is held in a shoe inside the stern locker, and about twelve inches above this a strong collar in the deck holds it secure. This mast carries the mizzen sail, which is very small but quite invaluable to us for reasons which will be obvious later. The foremast, which carries the mainsail on its vertical 'yard' or 'gaff', is much taller, and steps on deck in a metal shoe or 'tabernacle'. This mast is stayed by three wires, one to either side and one forward to the stem of the boat. The latter, the forestay, is spliced at the lower end into a terylene rope which passes through a single block at the stemhead, being then secured to a stout cleat on the foredeck. By easing off this rope lanyard, the mast falls backward to form a low ridgepole. It was seeing this mast forming a ridge over which a canvas cover was set that first gave me the idea of a tent.

By removing the bolt on which the foot of the mast pivots, and supporting the mast there on a three-foot-high 'crutch', at the same time unshipping the mizzen mast and replacing it with a shortened stump, I realised the mast could lie horizontally about three feet above the deck height to form a ridge pole. It had been a matter of moments to make the two supports when we bought the boat, and then a local tent-maker came and measured up for a stout white PVC-on-terylene tent which fitted over the entire boat.

"You must attach eyelets under her gunwale, or into the hull, to which the lower edge of the tent may be laced,' he advised, but the idea didn't appeal: I have a loathing of drilling any holes in boats' hulls for they are meant to keep water OUT, and any hole, no matter how protected, sooner or later lets water IN! For this reason I do not even have a drain-bung in *Lugworm*'s hull, preferring to rely on the well-tried method of hand bailing with a bucket. Suction bailers are good in racing dinghies, but not for craft which rarely sail at the speeds necessary for them to work, or which are to be left at anchor for long periods.

Instead of eyelets, therefore, I made up a stout terylene warp which can be rigged to encircle the hull about a foot below the gunwales, and it is to this that we lace down the bottom edges of the tent. This warp also serves as a strong girdle for hauling the boat up beaches, and when thus used has the advantage of taking the strain equally all round her hull in a gentle caress, rather than from one hard point such as a ringbolt.

The tent, when rigged, is high enough for us to sit comfortably on the top of the centreplate casing, though I must confess that it was not long before we were leaving the gaff and the mainsail laced to the mast even when it was in use as a ridgepole. Certainly this reduced the headroom a bit but did at least get the gaff and sail neatly out of the way. The mizzen mast, with the sail rolled round it, stows along one of the side-decks – if it isn't left on the beach.

Entry into the 'Christmas pudding' is via the stern where either one or both of the flaps may be rolled back. It all works very well, and of course when the boat is anchored from her bow alone, the open end of the tent is always orientated away from the wind, a point which any camper will appreciate. In a Drascombe Lugger, the outboard ships down a 'well' inboard of the transom, and the boat may be powered with the tent still rigged – a fact which came in very handy on more than one occasion.

I'll sketch the Christmas pudding and you will see that the tent can be rolled towards the bow for any distance one pleases, to uncover a greater amount of the boat.

The whole contraption takes about fifteen minutes for the two of us to rig from scratch and one valuable property of that white PVC tent is that, in addition to being light inside, it also acts almost like a greenhouse: on cold nights the temperature within is always many degrees higher than outside. In Greece we had often found it too hot altogether, so made ourselves a very light cotton tent which secured between the two masts covering part of the cockpit only. Though it gave some privacy, it was of course not waterproof.

The two airbeds, sleeping bags, spare clothes, and my typewriter and papers, went into the forward locker, the hatch of which was made watertight. Provisions stowed in one of two after lockers which are long, narrow and separated by the rudder trunking and the foot of the mizzen mast. The other after locker, on port side, contained the three gallon petrol tank whose feedline passed through a water-tight collar in the deck

CHRISTMAS PUDDING

above. Other non-perishable items such as foghorn, radar re-flector, underwater goggles and flippers, containers of spare oil for the fuel, tools and the like, also went into this locker.

On deck, right aft, we carried two two-gallon spare petrol containers making our total fuel capacity seven gallons, and since the longshaft Mercury outboard at cruising revs ran for about 2½-3 hours on a gallon this gave us a range of at least 70 miles at four knots, which is about the speed we would aver-age in calm water. This four horsepower motor, of course, was intended only as an auxiliary for when there was no wind or for shifting around in harbours; if there was an adverse wind it was hardly powerful enough to push us against it, and I do want to emphasise that *Lugworm* is essentially a sailing dinghy. Her centreboard – 120 lb. of galvanized steel plate – when fully lowered increased the draught to 3½ ft., and the steel rudder extended about eighteen inches below the hull also.

This rudder is unusual. It slots down through that narrow waterproof trunking you can see below it in the diagram, and the tubular metal rudderpost is attached to the tiller by a brass hinge at its upper end. The tiller therefore may be lifted up vertically out of the way, and when so lifted allows the rudder to swing through 360 degrees. You may wonder why I mention this, but it is very useful, for when the mizzen alone is set and sheeted home, the boat can be left to drift slowly stern-first while keeping her bows into any breaking seas. The rudder blade then 'trails' and thus one may easily steer the boat at the same time. I cannot think of any dinghy in which I would rather have tackled this cruise – and I have spent many thousands of hours in various other small craft.

For 'ready-use' lockers B. had the bright idea of fixing netting shelves, with stout elastic shock-cord at the inboard edge, tight up under the cockpit side-decks. I have attempted to show these in my drawing by cutting away a bit of the side-deck on the starboard side aft. In this netting we kept the chart in use at the time, distress signals, toilet gear and change of clothing plus the ever ready oilskins. Four gallons of fresh water was stowed in two plastic containers, and these together with a stainless steel two-burner alcohol pressure stove also stowed away under the side decks. With this and a full store of provisions we reckoned to be independent of 'civilisation' for about four days.

For ground tackle we carried two twelve pound Admiralty pattern anchors, one with 150 ft. of floating warp (¾ in. circumference) stowed on the foredeck, and the other with 90 ft. of 1½ in. circumference terylene stowed aft. We also carried an 18 in. diameter canvas sea-anchor, a complete spare set of standing and running rigging, and a spare jib and mainsail. The outfit was completed by a pair of eight foot oars which stowed one along either side of the foredeck. I can tell you when that lot was stowed away in the boat, plus the two of us, *Lugworm* floated an inch or two lower than the designer intended. But she has a very good sheer, with high bow, and even so overladen is a remarkably fine seaboat.

You may guess that wherever it took place, the transformation of a very lovely boat with her black hull and carved teak quarter-badges into a close resemblance to a Christmas pudding caused much amusement among the interested watchers. But she made a snug, dry little home, and the sky that evening in Othonoi gave every hint that we would need one before the night was out.

It rained; by Heaven it deluged again! As we lay on our air-beds, one down either side of the centreboard casing, with two candles throwing shadows in the warm yellow light, the thrumming of water on the tent made conversation almost impossible. It was like being inside a drum. Each of us lay with our own thoughts, that first night aboard of the great voyage home, and I know that I, for one, could not tear them away from the coming crossing to Italy. The night is not the best of times to consider such things; not when there's a first class thunderstorm with all its orchestration of acoustics putting in the background atmosphere. We resolved to stay put until this touchy weather had worked itself to other parts and we listened to the Greek weather forecast in English with much attention each morning and evening. It was just audible on our tiny transistor.

The following day proved clear with a brisk gusty wind from the north west, so together we explored the village and the entire island which is only about two and a half miles in length and less across. There are no roads worth the name: a rubble track leads from the harbour alongside a tamarisk hedge past the Church and the policeman's house and opens out into a wide area bounded on the seaward side by the pebble strand, and inland by a miscellany of spartan houses and the typical

Greek taverna – meeting place and social centre of the village. We wandered through the village and up the track which climbed the western side of the valley, for through the olive groves we had spied the roofs of a second village. It was just another small group of houses, with a taverna into which we went for a cup of the delicious strong black coffee. The day was warm and the climb had been steep – it was good to rest.

In a small community such as this, the visit of a strange boat – most especially a boat as strange as ours – is an event of note. It is certain that the word had already passed around that these two mad English were sailing home in their cockleshell, and while the Greeks are by nature far too polite and courteous to impose unwanted attention on a visitor, we sensed there was tremendous interest latent in the air, and before we had been seated in the taverna more than a minute or two, three islanders came in, ostensibly to order coffee, but really to size us up.

'*Kalimera,*' we opened the conversation, with the familiar greeting.

'*Kalimera sas,*' came the rejoinder. '*Ti kanete?*'

'Very well, thank you.'

The ice was broken; questions could flow. Was it true we proposed sailing to Italy? Had we come from Corfu? How old were we, and had we any children? What did we think of Greece? Was I a sailor? A navy man?

Always that triggered off reminiscences of the last war, for this subject is still very much alive in the minds of these people. One of the three, a large sensitive man, gripped my arm intensely. 'My brother,' he said. 'You are my brother; my own brother was in our merchant navy and the Germans ...' He was now beside himself with emotion. 'The Germans, in a submarine, they sank his ship, no guns they had, nothing ... they

28

sank his ship and he was drowned.' He broke down completely, tears streaming down his face, and the other two gently piloted him away while the proprietress of the taverna indicated that he was perhaps a little simple, but a good man, and it was very very sad.

We left more than a little downcast that the memories of so many years gone by should still be so near the surface, ready to spring up and raise again the bitterness and hatred which that war had left in its wake. We had heard this tale and similar a hundred and more times in country, town and island as we travelled around Greece, and knew that in one generation at least the roots of their sorrow and bitterness went deep, and there was no forgiving.

But it was difficult to remain sad on such a lovely and exciting morning. We set off up the gravel track towards the north of the island, facing the brisk wind that funnelled down the valley. Soon we were above the village, looking back from the shoulder of the hillside to where the top of *Lugworm*'s tent just poked above the wall in the distant harbour, and beyond that across a stretch of white-flecked sea, the hazy coastline of Corfu could just be seen.

Below us the rich green valley, clothed with pine and cypress, olive, fig and flowering broom, climbed on up to a table land of scrub and rocks. This gained, we wandered through thickets of wild thyme, thistles, and blackberry bushes towards the western shore, and finally stood on the edge of bluff cliffs looking across towards Italy, hopeful perhaps of making out some faint outline of her mountains; but there was nothing.

It was while scrambling up a further rise to view the island's coast northward that we met an islander who, rather oddly, seemed ill at ease and stood in our path as though reluctant at first to let us pass.

'That chap didn't want us to come up here,' I remarked to B. 'It was on the tip of his tongue to say "go back", but he didn't quite make it. Wonder what's afoot?'

We were not long in doubt. As we breasted the rise, which led to a gentle slope down to more cliff edges, we could see dotted about among the rocks a number of pigeon traps, and they are worth describing for their ingenuity. Each one of them consisted of a shallow hole scooped in the earth and on one edge of this a heavy flat rock was balanced so that, if allowed to do so, it would drop and cover the hole. On the opposite side of this hole another sharp edged piece of stone was placed and over the fulcrum edge of this a specially cut twig was balanced. A second twig sharpened at one end was lodged by its point against the upper end of the fulcrum twig, its far end jammed against the top of the balancing rock. From the lower end of the fulcrum twig two more twigs suitably shaped and sharpened were then jammed against the base of the rock. The slightest touch on any of the three spanning twigs resulted in the fulcrum twig being dislodged which immediately let the rock drop. A few beads of corn are put into the hole and the trap is ready. This island abounds in small very quick flying wild pigeons and the bird is a great favourite in the stew pot. When attempting to peck up the corn it inevitably triggers off the trap, and though cruel, they are evidently efficient, for on more than one occasion back in the village, we saw the trapper returning with his booty. I deliberately triggered one to see how difficult it was to reset and it was a tricky task. The object is to stun the bird and pin it down.

I remember as we wandered back later that evening, coming across a riot of white anemones with brilliant yellow centres, and there were orchids, iris (both blue and brown) and a type of mulberry bush. Indeed, some of the sheltered parts of the

PIGEON TRAP

island were like a natural garden, alive with swallows, and the occasional comical brightly coloured hoopoe, as well as small pigeon.

We ate in the taverna that night – a single room embodying a general store in addition to two wooden tables and a miscellany of hard chairs and benches. The island cooking was, well – distinctive. Apart from the occasional pigeon stew the staple diet appears to have been local fish deep fried or grilled in olive oil, with chips. Always chips; and this night I was strangely unsettled both in mind and stomach. While the meal was being prepared I looked around the room: piles of household wares, brooms, galvanized pails, plastic buckets, twine, and sacks of dried provisions were stacked about. The proprietor, an elderly wizened little man thin as a wraith and the colour of parchment, evidently suffered acutely from ulcers for he constantly groaned, was assailed by spasms of dry coughing, and had recourse to a bottle of what we assume was stomach pills. His wife, a quiet little body, dressed completely in black of the peasant costume, seemed to be in charge, and did the cooking. To our surprise, however, the two plates were brought in by a young man carrying a broken sports gun over one arm, who had obviously just returned from a shooting sortie in the hills, for behind him came an inquisitive black dog of the labrador variety. The sight of two unexpected strangers sitting in the room set him barking at full blast, and only when he had been forcibly removed did I learn that the youngster was the son of the house, and a fisherman to boot. This was fortunate, for we were able to clear up a small, but vital, navigational problem which had been worrying us. Our proposed track from Othonoi to Otranto in Italy, 295 degrees True, was plotted on a very small scale chart covering the entire Eastern Mediterranean. The crease where this chart folded partly obliterated what might have been a small cross, which is the symbol for a submerged rock, and this lay just north of our track line some few miles out to sea. Inspection of local Greek charts in Corfu revealed nothing of the sort in that area, but here was a fisherman who would certainly know if it existed.

Once he grasped my query – which was not easy with our limited means of communication – he disappeared behind the shop counter and shortly emerged with a battered large scale Greek chart of the local waters. Together we pored over this, and I learned much from its more detailed presentation of the island's coastline, but there was evidently no rock out there at sea. We sipped the bitter resinated wine, and picked away at the meal, and the conversation fell into desultory exchanges; but somehow I could not settle to enjoy the evening, and feeling a little sick, eventually excused myself with a remark to B. that I was going outside to have a look at the weather.

I remember sitting in the darkness on the bench under an old tamarisk tree before the taverna, and looking up at the fast scudding clouds. In the bright moonlight they seemed to leap from behind the hills, glance down at me, microscopic mortal that I was, laugh, and hurry on over the wild void of the sea. I looked out across that blackness of water, flecked with the fast moving silver patches which disappeared so quickly and gradually a dreadful weight of doubt seemed to envelop me like a shroud.

'What on earth are you doing here,' the voice of my reason seemed to ask … 'on this desolate place in the middle of an alien sea? Are you really going to hazard your own life and that of your wife, on that dark and lonely waste, where no man's hand can help if things go amiss?'

'You are a professional seaman,' the small insistent voice continued. 'You know full well that the first and most important rule is never to tempt Providence by taking unnecessary risks; true, your boat is sound and has a stout heart; but you do not need me to remind you of what will happen if the weather turns foul out there halfway to Italy. You know she is too small to take those seas which can rise within an hour to swamp her and send you both to a cold and lonely oblivion: be sensible now while you have the chance; once committed it may be too late.'

I rose, more disturbed than I cared to admit, and looked down at the beach, bright now in a moving patch of moonlight. The roar of the breakers below, and the sigh of a fitful squally wind rustling the trees in the valley behind seemed to voice an insistent warning. Far along the strand, glistening in the brief silver light, I could see the low stone wall of the harbour. Great God! Our boat was too small even to show above it, and as I looked the whole world seemed to expand, and I to shrink, until I was nothing more than a grain of sand in an immense and powerful cosmos which might, with no more effort than an idle shrug, dismiss me and all I held dear to nothingness.

Behind me the taverna window was a small but warm glow in the darkness. Inside there, I thought, was another who had committed herself to this venture simply for love of me, and for whom in this situation I was totally responsible. 'Be honest,' the voice within insisted, 'to risk your own life is your affair entirely; but to deliberately risk another's …'

I am not ashamed of these thoughts. I am a sailor, and well know the power and the loneliness of the sea. Many times, from the decks of all manner of large well-found ships I have watched grey wastes of water gathering in anger; watched in awe as mountains of energy, rolling invincibly from horizon to horizon, have begun to break and roar before the storm, and I know that a man plays with the sea on the sea's terms, and when his luck runs out, there is no bargain to be struck, no second chance.

The click of the latch on the taverna door broke my reverie. Silhouetted in the light I saw B. peering out into the dark. 'Ken,' she called, 'are you there?'

'Here under the tree,' I answered, and she walked over and sat beside me.

'A penny?' she asked, after a moment.

'Just thinking.'

'Out with it, then,' she said.

34

But it isn't easy, when it comes to it, to risk calling off a whole planned venture such as this. Still; what was in my mind had to be voiced.

'B.,' I said, 'we have talked of this often before, but I've got to be absolutely sure. When we set off into that void out there, we take a calculated risk, and if things turn against us, it is quite possible that we shall pay with drowning. It is very easy while sitting here safe ashore to feel it's a risk worth taking, but we both know that if it comes to it, we shall be alone to face the fact and there will be no help. It will be up to us and there will be no one to blame but me. Are you prepared to risk it?'

I swallowed hard. If she said 'No', then I knew I was bound to cancel the voyage there and then.

Straight came the answer. 'If that's all you're worrying about, yes, I am prepared to risk it. Of course I'm afraid; I'm terrified of what might happen, but I'm prepared to take the risk this once. To do it often would be foolish, but I think we can make the risk acceptable by watching the weather carefully. It may only take twelve hours – with a bit of normal luck.'

Suddenly my world shrank back to its normal size; I was batting again with as good a chance as the next man, and felt as though a tremendous weight had lifted from my shoulders. So later that night together we poured a small libation of wine over the end of the sea wall – for Neptune – and both slept like logs.

We watched the weather pattern like hawks. Intermittent squalls gave way to short calm periods with sunshine, but I was uneasy at the unsettled quick changes.

The following Sunday, however, our fourth day on the island, broke calm with not a cloud in sight and just a kiss of light southerly wind. A sea, still running from the recent brisk winds, was tailing off, and all looked fair for an evening start.

You may ask why we were prepared to choose a night crossing of the remaining 48 miles to Otranto, and the reason is simply that in these waters if the evening is calm there is a good chance of the whole night remaining so, whereas a calm dawn can, with the rising of the sun, bring violent winds by noon. There was a further reason: the probable time for the crossing, allowing an average speed of four knots (which is merely a guess anyway), would be somewhere around twelve hours, and in a dinghy I would much prefer to make an arrival on an unknown coast with the coming of daylight, rather than as night approaches or in darkness. You can then look for a quick lee rather than be forced to keep the sea if the weather turns foul. I therefore reckoned a start around 2100, wind or no wind, would be right and was prepared if necessary to use the motor rather than hang about becalmed far offshore. There were to be no heroics on this first crossing; the object was to get to Italy; plenty of time for disaster after that.

But the 1915 forecast in English from Athens Radio was so unexpected that we looked at each other and could not help laughing; never before during the whole preceding summer or winter had we heard the magic words 'All Greek seas will be calm.'

'Good old Neptune!' cried B. in what I suppose is the twentieth century equivalent of an Homeric Ode. Within an hour we were clear of the bay with a sweet northerly zephyr pressing genoa, main and mizzen as we filled on starboard tack towards the dark horizon.

Ah, but that was a moment! A half moon peered inquisitively down through a thin veil of haze, and the occasional star showed in clearer patches of sky as the outline of our island grew dim astern, finally to merge and disappear altogether in the blackness. Only the moving beam from the lighthouse remained arcing regularly across the sky to assure us there was still solid land in our lonely world of water. Within a couple of hours that too became a faint yellow glowworm, a mere yardstick to dimension, before capitulating to the void.

'Goodbye Greece,' I thought, and noted the time. It was nearly midnight and we were alone, an immense outrageous speck in a void of nothingness that seemed to be considering us quietly, tongue-in-cheek.

If you have never been alone in a very small boat on a very large sea, and at night, then you may never have had the opportunity of viewing yourself in true perspective with the universe. I do not speak of size only, but of values and of such considerations also as human destiny.

In such a situation, and if misfortune should catch you fully aware, you may see yourself as balanced on a tightrope of life, poised unwillingly and precariously between the illusions of Heaven and Hell, Beginning and End. If you then dare to scan that dark ocean which has no shores, you may also have the courage to realise how diverting it is to construct a shadow-harbour called meaning – you may even fool yourself that you glimpse a Hand that jerks the puppet-strings, imagining even that it points out to you a horizon beyond which lies Truth. But that is a disastrous course to lay, for it will rock the ship of sanity too violently for contemplation; and this, after all, is only an account of a terrestrial voyage in this strange experience called life, so bring your eyes to the compass again and try to keep that star ahead in comfortable proximity to the shroud: it may guide us through this night at any rate.

So the long hours went by, the moon swung visibly aside, and still the sea slept, fanned by that soft north wind, and *Lugworm* sang a very quiet song that chuckled and swirled astern, to which a living path of phosphorescence danced. There was

37

no other ship, or boat, or life on that whole immensity of dark sea, save one small bird that burst with an explosion of wing-beats to settle and share our void for one brief moment, then left us to an even greater solitude.

We slept for an hour at a time, wrapped in a sail and lying on the cockpit floor. After a while the wind fell so light that I started the outboard, and the dull monotony of its throbbing made it all the more difficult not to be hypnotised by sleep, but still the faint breeze gave us a little help from the sails, and it was more than an hour later that, drowsily peering ahead, my attention focused on one spot.

Reaching down, I softly shook B. 'Look,' I said, pointing into the blackness over our port bow, 'and count.' Vague as a wish, a finger of not-so-dark seemed to rise, beckon, then fall again. Time and again we watched; was it three times every fifteen seconds? There was no further doubt: it was the loom of the light on Cape Santa Maria di Leuca – a bright spur on the very tip of Italy's heel down there far far over the horizon. Quickly I took a bearing; if our average speed of four knots was accurate the circle of visibility of the light coupled with our estimated distance run indicated that our position was slightly south of the trackline; we altered another five degrees northward and within half an hour we picked up a second light straight over the bow. It was Cape Otranto, our landfall, over twenty miles away.

I don't really know what either of us expected to sight when Italy first swum out of the lightening dawn, but for me it was a surprise. Accustomed as we had been for the last ten months to the hard rocky mountain-tops of the Greek Islands, bunching almost in defence against the blue sea, this long level coast ahead belonged to a different world. Low ochre-coloured cliffs shone gold in the first shaft of morning sun, stretching either way to north and south. They seemed, wordlessly, to speak of the vast continent behind, where land, land and more land rolled endlessly back. 'I can afford,' they seemed to be saying, 'to lose a few million acres to this tiny sea every year. There is plenty more of me back there.'

We hove up at 0630 in fifty feet of water close under a russet coloured cliff and no sooner had *Lugworm* settled to her anchor than a clamour of black crows launched in protest from scores of holes lining the cliff top. With one mind they swooped, spread their wings and jettisoned a cargo of good luck all over us and the boat.

'Don't fret,' I comforted B., wiping a well aimed tribute out of her hair. 'It's only the ghosts of drowned sailors jealously reminding us how lucky we have been.'

'Maybe, but I think it's a pretty poor entry into the Common Market,' she answered.

It's very hard to be poetic with B. in the boat.

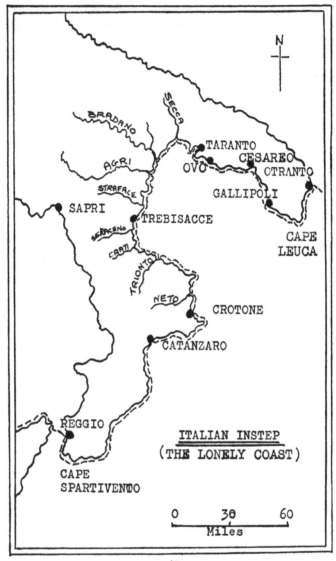

ITALIAN INSTEP
(THE LONELY COAST)

CHAPTER II

The Lonely Coast

OTRANTO WAS OUR NEAREST official 'port of entry' into Italy, hence the need to make a landfall some twenty-five miles north of Cape Santa Maria di Leuca, round which we were bound to sail anyway. It was a great challenge trying to speak Italian after ten months struggling with Greek especially since my own mastery of the language was contained within the first four lessons of a Linguaphone course taken fifteen years before. B. was in even worse state, though later it was she who became more competent; it's something to do with age.

We brewed up a cup of coffee there under the cliffs, wiped the dew and the good-luck off the decks and stowed the boat neatly before nosing into the sleepy harbour. Before long we were confronting the Customs Officers. Fortunately one of these, a tall goodlooking chap, spoke a little English and after glancing at the dossier marked 'Ship's Papers' which I presented, he surveyed us quizzically and then strode to the window through which *Lugworm* was visible.

'You have come from Corfu,' he stated, 'and you are sailing to England.' I nodded. He glanced for a moment at his assistant and then gathering up the folder moved towards the door, beckoning us to follow. 'I must examine your "ship",' he said with faint emphasis on the last word, and my heart fell – not because we had anything to conceal but at the thought of what such officialdom might portend along the vast seaboard which lay ahead. Never once in Greece had we been officially inspected other than in amusement or natural curiosity. It seemed we were now suspect.

Aboard the boat the officer and his assistant sat in the cockpit and looked about them. I caught the glance of one of them when he came face-to-face with Foogoo – who was giving every bit as good as he got. And then, 'What have you in there?' he asked pointing to the forehatch. 'Clothes, our bedding, my typewriter, paper and things' I replied. 'And in there?' he pointed to the two after hatches, adding, 'I would like to see in them.' The two of them got down on the floorboards and with bottoms in the air squinted into the narrow lockers which were crammed with foods and equipment. They then peered up through the netting under the side-decks, felt the furled sails, examined the outboard, fingered the rigging wires and tested the weight of the oars, chattering meanwhile in voluble Italian. Finally the assistant attempted to lift one of the cockpit floorboards, and this is no easy task. 'Truly,' I said, feeling a thorough criminal, 'really we have no dutiable stores aboard.' Unless B. was engaged in a bit of private dope smuggling, I knew we were innocent of all else. The senior official looked at me. 'But we do not doubt it,' he smiled. 'It is just that we cannot understand – where do you keep the mad dogs?'

After that things were much happier. Back in the Customs House we were issued with our first real 'ship's paper' in the form of a magnificent *Constituto in Arrivo per il Naviglio da Diporto* to put in our folder and I swear *Lugworm* wagged her tail as we filed it away in the ship's office – under the airbeds in the fore locker. Those two officials proved real friends, helping us to translate the weather forecasts, and identifying the stations on our minute tran-sistor against the wavebands on their own sophisticated equipment.

But a rapidly blackening sky portended no good and by noon the wind had freshened a lot. We rigged the tent and set off to explore the coast southward on foot.

Some of the most interesting landmarks right round the coast of Italy are the 'Torres' – watchtowers – built long ago to guard against approaching danger in the form of pirates and the like. These lookout towers formed a chain, usually within sight of one another, from which signals might be passed. Built very solidly of stone, some of them have been kept in fine condition, indeed on occasion we found them converted into splendid private houses, while others are mere mounds with only a few cut blocks indicating their original use.

Torre dell'Orto, for instance, a mile south of Otranto, is almost totally demolished, only one section of its circular walls still standing.

We knew from our voyaging around Greece that, taking into account enforced stops due to bad weather and days spent exploring ashore, we could expect to average about twelve miles a day in the boat. Of course, sometimes we quadrupled this distance when conditions were good, but the great safety factor about this voyage was the length of time available; there was no need to rush – and that meant no need to take risks with the weather. I am convinced that this time factor is the cause of many disasters in small boat cruising. When there is a date looming up which must end the cruise, or any urgency to be in one place at a given time, even the most experienced seaman tends to take more risks than he would otherwise.

This is not meant as an indictment of racing – then one must expect to take risks, and long may there be people courageous enough to accept these risks – that's the challenge of it. But when cruising quite different priorities apply. Indeed on this trip home we must have walked almost as far as we sailed, for always when pinned down in a place of refuge we used the time to survey the coast ahead. In our situation it was comforting to know beforehand that just beyond some rocky headland there lay a small beach where the boat might be grounded; or that halfway along a ten mile stretch of unbroken sand was an inlet leading perhaps to a tiny lagoon. So often the chart, in these minor and normally unimportant details, proved lacking. For us, thirty feet or so of shingle beach jammed between miles of cliffs and rocks might spell the difference between safety and disaster.

The following morning the forecast gave strong southwesterly winds of force six to seven. The sea, so calm twenty-four hours before was already a forbidding picture and obviously it was a day for exploration.

I remember that first long walk in Italy well, and for a most unusual reason. Beyond the lighthouse on Cape Otranto the straight low cliffs gave way to a more indented rockier shore backed by hills. It was while wandering round a small inlet called Porto Badisco two miles south of the light that we came across heaps of dead seaweed, piled up like brown straw just above the waterline. That's what we thought it was until, when taking to a small coast road a few hundred yards beyond we were intrigued at the sight of detached pieces of this 'weed' walking across the metalled surface. Each small piece of raffia-like weed was steering a course unerringly up wind. Indeed, it was clear that no other course was possible, for the trailing

fronds of straw, looking like miniature witches' brooms, blew
to leeward and the grub, whose perambulating parts were all
at the bow, crawled doggedly on totally guided by the air-
stream. Whether these creatures had inhabited the dead weed,
or whether the whole insect had assumed an identical form by
way of camouflage, it was quite impossible to tell, though the
latter seemed more likely. The closest examination betrayed no
joint of grub and weed: it all seemed to be one. I'll draw it with
my toe beside to give an idea of size.

WEED INSECT,
WITH TOE ADJACENT.

We knew that our first place of safety was the tiny fishing
harbour of Porto Castro twelve miles from Otranto, and the
following noon put to sea under all sail before a light northerly
and ran close down the shore to enter this tiny port in the early
evening. We found it to lie just west of a small pointed headland snug under the cliffs, and to consist of two quite separate
inlets, too small for anything but open day boats. The eastern
harbour is formed by a stone breakwater running out almost
parallel to the cliff with a quay on its inner side, and it was to
this that we berthed, stern-to.

It is interesting to dwell on the reaction of fisherfolk to our
appearance in such remote harbours – we came to expect a cer-

tain pattern of behaviour, and soon began to understand the causes. Unless we obviously needed help – in which case it was always willingly given – there would first be an almost studied indifference; as though the locals wished to imply that the appearance of a strange boat was of no account whatever, and they would all carry on with their business almost deliberately not meeting one's eye, or in any way making contact. Very shortly, however, when we were safely berthed under the watchful but guarded observation of all present (did this foreigner know how to handle a boat?), and when we had left *Lugworm* perhaps to explore the port, one would see a group collect on the quay alongside the boat. She would then be subjected to curious and very detailed scrutiny. If we returned towards the boat the group would usually disperse, but now faces would not be averted, eyes would meet, a small measure of contact might casually be made. I knew this was the moment to ask for some form of assistance, for there is no finer or quicker way of making friends than placing one's self at a small disadvantage; country people and fishermen, as individuals, are almost without exception, kind. The art lies in knowing how to present an opportunity for the individual to overcome the barrier of fear – fear of a rebuff from the stranger, fear of inviting the censure of his own group by appearing to be too friendly with those who, after all, might turn out to be objectionable. It would be either the strongest character of the group – the natural leader – or the buffoon who volunteered to exchange any pleasantries, or more likely pass some good-natured humorous comment at the expense of the stranger, ostensibly to make his companions laugh, but in reality to sound out the newcomers' reactions. All this, however, could be short circuited by a well-timed appeal for information, or a request for help to moor the boat or an offer to buy something. Show one's self to be a human be-

ing, endowed with similar reticences and an errant soul like all
others present, and the barriers would fall, questions flood in.
From that moment on, the atmosphere would be one of ready
help and genuine interest. The fact that one small man and this
slight woman (B. never failed to soften the hardest hearts for
she has an appealing shyness and delicacy with strangers) had
come in this tiny boat so like their own all the way from Greece
– Goodness! And bound for Taranto? Could it be true – right
round the Cape! To Reggio – NEVER! That was round the toe
of Italy itself!

England. England? Where exactly was England ... that was
the other side the world somewhere, eh? Again and again in
southern Italy astonishment would be shown at the crossing from Greece, whereas our intention of sailing to England
brought nothing more than a nod. It was too far away to mean
anything.

*   *   *

As you swan southward towards the very tip of Italy's heel the
coast becomes progressively more rocky and steep, climbing
straight from the water's edge four hundred feet and more up
pine clad hills. That next week sailing before a brisk northerly,
we were able to run within yards of the cliffs, poking into every
grotto and tiny bay hungry for what might be revealed; and
it was a surprise when suddenly the domed top of the lighthouse on Cape Leuca loomed above the limestone hillside. It
grew taller and taller as we circled the headland until finally the
whole eight-sided column towered graceful and white into an
unbelievably blue sky for all the world like a colossal needle left
sticking in a green and white pin cushion having sewn together
the blue Adriatic and the wine-dark Ionian. Banks of terraced
steps led from the little harbour up the hillside to the church of

Santa Maria di Finibus Terrae – Our Lady of Land's End – for such was the ancient Latin name of this headland from which sailors since time im-memorial have taken bearings when voyaging from Greece to Sicily.

We rounded the point and beat up into the shelter of the mole, well protected from the north but very vulnerable to the dreaded Sirocco winds that come scorching up from Africa. There was no room at the quayside for a stranger; indeed the local fishing boats seemed hard put to find space. So we sailed a little westward towards Punta Ristola and brought up in a small shallow cove with a sandy beach at its head.

I recall that evening sketching one of the fishermen weaving a beautifully delicate but functional lobster pot from thin split bamboo cane. It stood about five feet high when finished and was light as thistledown. He told me that he made one every two days and I believed him for his fingers wove the cane with incredible dexterity. Later we saw boats putting to sea laden with these basket pots piled high and looking rather like floating haystacks.

But a major decision now had to be made; whether to sail the seventy or so miles direct across the Gulf of Taranto to Crotone, or to continue coasting three times that distance round the instep. For reasons already explained, the former course was very risky, especially since this area is noted for its sudden and violent storms. On the other hand, for the next three hundred and more miles, the coast, apart from the three ports of Gallipoli, Taranto and Crotone, offered virtually no shelter until we were round the toe of Italy and into Reggio, Calabria. From inspection of the chart it was evident that rivers flowed into the sea at fairly evenly spaced intervals, but whether these would be navigable even in so small a craft as ours was problematical, and we got very conflicting answers to our queries

THE LOBSTER POT MAN

on this point. Obviously if we did creep round the coast, the two of us alone might need to get *Lugworm* up the beaches if necessary and above the breaker level.

'If we went direct and conditions remained fine, we could be in Crotone within twenty-four hours,' I mused, watching B. to see her reaction.

'Yes, but to get caught out across the mouth of the Gulf with nearest land over thirty miles away would make us look pretty

49

silly,' was her sensible comment. To be honest the weather was worrying us both. For the time of year it seemed all wrong. A choleric purple haze, not to mention intermittent rumbles of thunder back inland was more akin to late summer than early spring, and recent disturbed conditions made us wary of sudden violent storms.

So the decision was taken: round the coast it would be. Now I must tell you that fully laden *Lugworm* weighs something around 1,200 lb. and this is more than one man and a slip of a girl can haul up a beach. While in Greece we had devised a method of getting the boat on to a lee shore above the breakers, provided that this was effected before those breakers became large enough to swamp the craft. Success depended on making the decision to land in good time, but the system itself was simple. Having selected a suitable spot where the beach appeared to slope gently and the waves were not too violent, we would drop our bow anchor and lie head-to-seas just outside the breakers with mizzen alone set and sheeted hard. Our tent girdle of floating rope was then rigged round the entire hull and a double block attached aft. With outboard and centreplate raised, and the rudder unshipped, B. would then station herself at the bow and start checking away on our 150 ft. of anchor warp while I stood at the stern with the second anchor and 90 ft. of terylene warp, the end of which was already rove through one sheave of the double block. As *Lugworm* drifted back I would wait for the first crunch on the beach, then leap ashore taking the anchor and the warp-end with me. Then came the tricky part. You will realise that it was essential to keep the boat bow to sea, for to broach across the waves might easily have meant swamping. While B. kept the bow warp taut, I would jam the stern anchor behind some convenient rock ledge or even round the bole of a tree, then, with a rolling hitch, attach a single block to the warp about halfway up the beach. Through this single block I would reeve the tail end of the stern warp, then take it quickly through the second sheave of the double block at *Lugworm*'s stern: which sounds simple, but try doing it with the boat lifting and sheering in the white water, and often a long surge running up and down the shingle.

Taking the strain on the tackle I would haul *Lugworm*'s stern hard ashore while B., having eased off a suitable amount on the bow warp and turned up, would leap ashore and join me on the tackle. It all had to be worked with a keen eye to the seas and surge and *Lugworm*'s angle relative to both, but having used a surge to get her as high as possible up the beach, there would then be brief periods of respite, for she would only 'lift' at the very top of each following surge. We had time to look around for some likely piece of driftwqod to jam under her keel aft, over which the boat could more easily slide, for you will realise that dragging her across soft sand (this was the worst of all) or fine shingle was, even with the tackle, very difficult. Once a flat rock, or maybe a stout piece of driftwood, was positioned there, we would together get down to the heavy work of dragging her further back. Even with the tackle it was not easy, but half a boat's length was often sufficient, for it was only necessary that she be above the line where the longest surge might float her. Of course, if we proposed leaving the boat for any time we would make sure she was well above the danger line, bearing in mind that an increase of wind might well bring the surge another fifteen to twenty feet up the beach.

It was the first of May before the weather relented from a minor tantrum of squalls and heavy rain, giving us leave to continue up the coast to Gallipoli. We covered thirty miles that day, mooring just after sundown in the shallow western basin of the old port. I shall never forget our first sight of the place as we rounded Punta del Pizzo three miles to the south. It was one of those evenings when the world has lost her brash reality and taken on the gentle miraculous colours of a Turner or Ruskin. Distances grew immense, expanding under the soft rose and green of an evening sky and the old town seemed to float above the edge of the sea, shimmering over the fortified walls, and marvellously heightened by the mirage effect. We were still too far off to make out the narrow low causeway that joins it to the modern extension on the mainland. It hovered there, the last shafts of sunlight glowing on the western walls, and we just sat and drank it in, ghosting silently up before a soft south wind, half afraid that it would evaporate before our eyes like some dream citadel; it was not without cause that the ancient Greeks named her Kallipolis – Beautiful City.

But that magical quality endowed by distance was soon dispelled as we landed on her busy quays, for it was market day, and we were soon lost in the hubbub of stalls, and noisy bargaining. Adjacent to the dock gates were the shellfish stalls, piled high with shrimps, mussels and oysters, to say nothing of scallops and cockles, crayfish and many types of winkles, B., to my astonishment, proclaimed that she had never tasted an oyster, so we bought three each and half a lemon, first getting the exuberant stallkeeper to open the shells for us, watched in amusement by a crowd who quickly gathered. Our arrival had not passed unnoticed from the walls towering over the basin, and the Red Ensign advertised our novelty value. That lively and uninhibited interest which is the hallmark of the Italians was soon unleashed on us, captives as we were, among the crowd. But we took our oysters along the quay, climbed some narrow worn steps directly above *Lugworm* and sat on the very top of the immense stone walls, savouring each mouthful as we watched the last light disappear over the east basin where the fishing boats were busy unloading.

It was exciting to later roam the busy streets of the new town across the causeway. The elections for a new government were taking place very shortly, and loudspeakers blazoned the virtues of various candidates – of which there seemed to be dozens – not without attendant noisy comments from the populace. But we were tired after a full day's sailing, and it was good to return aboard to the comparative peace of *Lugworm*, lulled until the early hours of the morning by the – for us – unusual distant noise of a large town.

*   *   *

A source of some contention between B. and myself is my built-in aversion to guide books. The truth is, I'm a born explorer – in a world where the art is well nigh impossible to exercise. Just show me a hill and I ask, 'Is there anything more interesting than what might lie over the top?' Drop me in the middle of a town and my day will be happily spent poking round each successive corner. So you will understand that, this waffling along unknown coastlines was pure bliss; for I can imagine no greater stimulation than not knowing what lay beyond the next headland. 'In Heaven's name,' I would argue with her, when in one of my more belligerent exploratory moods, 'who wants to wander about a stage, the "sets" of which are already "old hat" before you arrive? Surely, there's more fun in discovering things for one's self. Why ruin all the effect by knowing about it first?'

But this advanced form of philosophy falls on barren ground. 'In that case,' she might reply with decimating logic, 'why have you spent a fortune on Admiralty charts?' Indeed, it is difficult to be ethereal with B. She lives on a more realistic plane than I, and I love her for it, but there is some romantic quality lacking in her make-up – a fact which helps keep us solvent.

Anyway, about ten miles up the coast from Gallipoli the chart showed a shallow saltwater lake with narrow inlet from the sea. It looked interesting, especially since the lake was thicker with crosses than a churchyard. 'That's the place for tonight,' I assured her as we hoisted sails outside Gallipoli. 'If we miss all those rocks and provided we can get through the entrance, it'll make a magnificent shelter.' But I ought to have known better and left that first bit out.

'You mean Porto Cesareo?'

'Uh-huh' I commented, settling comfortably against the base of the mizzen mast. She continued to study the chart with more dedication than a crossword puzzle – and that's saying a lot for B.

'It's got "Occ. 3 sec. 13 M. La Salmenta. 92. conspic." in brackets. What's all that mean?' she queried after a long silence.

'Leading lights occulting every three seconds, visible for thirteen miles. Get them dead in line and they take you into the lake clear of all off-lying rocks. A transit of the two bears 034 degrees True,' I said taking a quick squint over her shoulder. 'Useful for checking your compass. La Salmenta must be a village with something conspicuous ninety-two feet high, probably a church, for taking bearings on.'

But I sensed she still wasn't happy. I had another look at the chart myself. True, it was a very tiny entrance, with no more than a fathom depth at the narrowest neck, which was fine so long as no swell was running, and it wasn't.

'It's a lousy lee shore,' she said after a while.

It was a gorgeous morning, very hot with a light westerly kissing the sails and *Lugworm* chuckling with bliss. We passed the Torres Sabea, Fiume, Caterina and Luzzio, bright against a darker line of hills beyond. I was stretched full length now deepening my tan, idly studying the outline of Gallipoli astern, which still quivered in the heat haze.

'Where do we go if we can't get in?' came the query.

'Oh, we'll find somewhere, there's sure to be some crack in the coast.'

Silence.

'We're heading straight for a wreck,' came the voice.

I never have established the cause, but B. just has these days. The strange thing is that they only occur when the weather is calm, hot, and doling out buckets full of Paradise: but let it turn foul, indeed bring on any emergency situation and she's as cool as a cucumber, competent up to her beautiful eyelashes. Maybe it's just a basic incompatibility of Nordic blood and Mediterranean humidity, but obviously this was to be one of those days.

'Don't worry about it, cuckoo.' I had noted that wreck marked on the chart and we were passing well inshore of it. As for Porto Cesareo I wasn't a bit worried: if the Italians took the trouble to mount leading lights on beacons, certainly they were not there to beguile mermaids; it was a safe bet the lake was used by local fishermen.

'Good God!'

I sat up. From B. that might mean anything, but she was still looking at the chart.

'Have you seen when this was last corrected? 5th February, 1954 – nearly *twenty years* ago!'

'All the more fascinating,' I consoled her. 'It shows what the coast was like then – intriguing to see the alterations in the last twenty years.' All the same, I thought, squinting at the chart, that did seem a bit antiquated.

'You're wrong, see, here,' and I pointed to the bottom left hand corner. 'Last small correction was in 1965. 1954 was the last large correction incorporated when the new edition of the chart was printed.'

'So it's only seven years out of date,' came the comment, not without sarcasm. 'The lake could still have silted up in that time: there may be no entrance at all.'

'Cuckoo, DO stop fidgeting. How do you think the early navigators coped when the chart simply ran out on them, imagine it: nothing but a dotted line and "UNSURVEYED" written in with a quill pen and splendid little fat cheeked cherubs puffing all over the place with their backsides obliterating five hundred miles of coastline that might or might not be there; how would you feel about that? Seven years – Hah! The sand hasn't settled on the barnacles yet.'

I might have saved my breath.

'And what's THIS,' she squeaked, unrolling the chart from gunwale to gunwale, 'CAUTION – SUBMARINE EXERCISE AREA. And we're slap in the middle of it!' She was standing now, bristling with alarm as though expecting at any moment to be impaled on a periscope.

'For heaven's sake, cuckoo, any submarine Commander who brought his vessel this near to the coast would need wheels on his bottom, just forget it, lie down and enjoy the sun.'

There was a long pause. 'Torpedoes!' came a faint squawk.

You see what I mean? I started ferreting about in the locker for a bag of tomatoes and the flask of wine. From experience I know the best thing in the circumstances is to feed her. But the trouble with those after lockers is they're long and narrow and in such a locker – have you noticed? – anything you want is always right at the back. I got down on all fours, the helm jammed under one elbow, and squinted into the cavern. Above me there was a flapping of terylene. I leapt up. Over the bow, Gallipoli was grinning at us. B. was sitting with tightly compressed lips, with an expression of long suffering. *Lugworm* was in irons.

'Back the jib please, darling,' I requested quietly. But we were already making sternway. The helm slammed over, knocking the wine bottle off the side-deck, the tomatoes were already spread over the chart, two of them squashed flat.

'Happy now, Vasco da Duxbury?' came the comment as we continued in a silent but profound dudgeon. But you must know that I have a buoyant soul, a soul that is nourished on sunshine, and I cannot respond to pique, even under the most extreme provocation.

Ahead the low coast swept in a splendid curve westwards, and somewhere along there forty miles away in the shimmering haze was the mighty port of Taranto. Exciting to think we would be there tomorrow – and after that? Nothing but the lonely coast, and rivers; truly, this was adventure.

The leading marks at Cesareo stood out clearer than Belisha beacons; two black and white chequered towers, one behind the other, and around them the sprawling chaos of a thriving town. 'See what I mean,' I cried to B. 'What can happen in a mere seven years – the place is throbbing with life. So much for your sanded up wilderness.' Indeed a high powered fishing boat was charging out of the narrow inlet, a white bone in her teeth and the whole navigational problem had evaporated: all one had to do was to stand on until those towers came in line, then steer for them.

We freed off and surged under sail through the narrow channel, the reefs glowering black on either hand, while beneath our keel the white sand was pock-marked with darker spots of weedy rock. Once clear inside the entrance I rounded head-to-wind and we handed all sail, for I thought it wiser to proceed under motor for the first time in this busy harbour. All secure we headed under power direct for a low stone quay. On the far side of the channel, along the sandy beach, a man was running, waving cheerily to us. I stood on the transom and returned his salutation, commenting happily on the splendid welcome.

Inertia is a strange thing. If you've ever daydreamed while going up a store's escalator you will know what I mean; there you are flat on your face in the haberdashery. But you try it balanced on a rocking deck with your eyes glued through the glasses on a running figure half a mile away. I can tell you that acceleration from a relative nil to four knots plus in zero time is devastating. Devastating enough to hammock B. in the foresail and send me crashing headlong in the cockpit.

'Astonishing,' she commented dryly, when the mess was sorted out and we had established *Lugworm* was undamaged. 'Astonishing how fast rocks can grow in seven years. But I do observe,' she added with icy sarcasm, 'that we were about a hundred yards off the transit when we hit.'

Dammit, with B. in the boat, a chap can't be perfect ALL the time.

*   *   *

To be honest, I think I like being lost. After all, one spends all one's lifetime being continuously 'found', getting lost makes a change. Now you might wonder how this is possible along a dead straight piece of coast when you know perfectly well that the port you've just left is back there behind you, and the port you're heading for is certainly within thirty miles or so ahead. But like most things in life being lost is a purely relative state. On that hot and oppressive morning it was relative to Cesareo and Taranto.

58

The trouble is, all those damned 'Torres' look the same. Oh, their names are wonderfully different: there's Torre Chianca and Torre Lapillo, Torre Colimena, San Pietro, Boraco and Molini all standing guard along that low Apulian coast and which, I ask you, is which? Just miss one, or see a hillock which might – or might not – tell its own sad story of ravage and rape, and where are you? You're frantically stabbing around with dividers and a clock. Not one of them flies a banner with its name blazoned on it, and anyway you can't keep checking when there's toast and marmalade and hot coffee to be made, and one ear clamped to the well-nigh incomprehensible weather forecast.

I realise now that everything was wrong for us that day we left Cesareo: we just ought to have stayed snugged up in that rocky lake, but to tell the truth B. had been so terribly bitten by gnats that it was a relief for both of us to get sails on *Lugworm* and feel a breath of fresh salt wind round our hides.

The forecast had been good: variable force three with possibility of thunderstorms and that was nothing new. If we'd taken any notice of thunderstorms we would still have been back in Otranto. Even so, I soon felt in my more arthritic joints that something might be brewing weatherwise. Inland, over the distant hills, there were the usual grumbles of thunder, but the wind was just too good to throw away; steady south-easterly; even a soldier might have put to sea. We bowled along under genoa, main and mizzen and life would have been blissful had it not been for B.'s continual scratching and the changing colour of the sky.

I must tell you about that south Italian sky, and had best start with a phrase we soon came to recognise as an old and clinging friend: for it was to come regularly out of our radio speaker: *Possibilita di temporale con locale colpi di vento*. Liberally translated, and depending on whether it was before or after breakfast, this had come, for us, to mean anything from 'possibility of thunderstorms with brisk winds locally' to 'watch it! freak storms with gale force winds'. That morning our barometer was steady at 994 – indeed it had been steady at 994 for so many days that I took to hitting it, hoping to see the blue needle move, whereas only the silver one fell off. But the sky! It began far inland over the hills, to turn a deep hazy purple. Gradually, outlined in the pyrotechnic display of sheet lightning we saw the hard black outline of thunder clouds seeming to grow without moving perceptibly. The odd thing was that they appeared to infuse into the air against the direction of the wind – calculated to give any sailor the jim-jams.

By 1000 there was an oppressive heat uncommonly like the Sirocco, but I prayed there was too much easterly in it for that. By 1030 that morning the sky all over was puce coloured, like an over-ripe victoria plum, and the wind still steady south-easterly was freshening, but what appalled me was the sudden appearance of a swell, rolling up from our quarter. Now if anything will make my hair stand on end, it is swell, for that spells finis to any thought of landing on an exposed beach, be it a lee or weather shore.

'Here B.,' I said, 'take the helm: I'm going to take a good look at the chart.' Being lost is all very well, but to Hell with it when you need to know where you are. Rapidly I worked back from the last known position; off Cesareo entrance at 0800. At just under four knots that put us about nine miles along the coast; Torre Colimena should be abeam. It wasn't. Mount della Marina, 374 ft., should be on the starboard bow, two miles inland. To my horror I realised that we could no longer see two miles inland for there was a thick wall of grey rain sweeping like an express train along the coast obliterating everything.

I grabbed the glasses and threw B. her oilskin. The beach, half a mile northward, was growing dim in the pall, but already I could see massive breakers pounding up the shingle and sand. Perhaps we could get in there, if we had to – but it would more than likely mean losing *Lugworm* for she would be swamped and rolled within seconds.

Hastily we stowed the chart and all perishable gear, battening down the locker hatches. The wind was still freshening as the first portentous splash of rain overtook us. Minutes later we were deluged in the roaring hissing storm, fighting to change the genoa for the small jib. I furled the mizzen sail and un-shipped its mast, laying the spar along the side deck to reduce windage aft, for when on the run like this it's not good to have too much pressure abaft the rudderpost. Then, with B. still manfully at the helm, and *Lugworm* fairly creaming down the now foaming seas, I started to reef the main. By the time all the reef-points were fast, and the sheet-block snapped into the leech reef-cringle, it was obvious that *Lugworm*, even reefed, would be over-canvassed. The wind was shrieking now, a wild dirge, and a glance astern was enough to set one praying; oceans of charging white crests, streaked and flattened by the scream-ing wind. Things didn't look good. 'O.K.?' I bellowed back to B. She smiled bravely, standing astride the helm, swaying against the roll of the boat, every nerve concentrating on keep-ing *Lugworm* steady before the rising seas; it was all happening far too quickly for my liking, this maelstrom. We had to get the jib off her, and quickly, but I did not like being off the helm any longer – one bad broach across these waves and I knew that we could be on nodding terms with the squids. I grabbed the helm. 'Get that jib off her,' I roared, 'and try to come back aft as quickly as possible – mustn't keep weight forward!' She cast off the halyard, then lay along the bucking foredeck to gather in the thrashing sail. For one moment I thought she must have cast off the wrong halyard, for incredibly the mainsail, too, was down and flogging across her out over the side. Then I knew: the mast itself had gone overboard.

In emergency you think of many things at once. Two thoughts were uppermost: is B. all right, and how could the mast have gone?

'Are you O.K.?' I bellowed, not daring to leave the helm. There was a muffled cry from under the sail. I could see her struggling to extricate herself. Thank God, she came out, white faced but unhurt. 'Back here,' I yelled, 'Here, on the helm, quick!'

There was no choice now, I had to get that sail and the spar inboard before it filled under water and made the boat uncontrollable. In it came, a tangle of terylene, wire and rope, and I just had time to see the four securing bolts of the tabernacle grinning at me – wrenched up, nuts and all through the massive king-plank, and then I was back on the helm and getting the outboard started, to regain control.

Lugworm, now shorn of all her glory, was riding the seas wonderfully. Astern the creamers reared and seemed to tower over us ready to burst down on deck and 'poop' us. But like a cork she would cock her tail up high, level off, and then as the crest foamed past, sink down again ready for the next; it was superb to watch. But this was no time for admiration: the decision had to be made – to bring her round head to wind and seas and get the sea-anchor out, deliberately stopping her further passage and trying to ride out the storm – or to continue as long as we dared under power and running before the wind in the hope of finding some lee?

When one is actually in the situation, this is a horrible decision to have to make. All one's instincts are to get the boat's bow into that wind, for she would then cleave the waves and throw them back on either side – but this meant staying at sea through whatever was still to come, and the look of the sky astern was enough to fill one with dread. The wind showed no signs of easing and the rain, driving horizontally, now blotted out the shore even close abeam, though we could still hear the thunder of breakers above the din. Believe me, when it comes to it, there is an overpowering desire to find a lee as fast as possible, and in our position that meant continuing to run under power.

Lugworm was still doing well. As long as we could prevent her broaching, and equally important prevent her actually surfing down the steep seas, we would survive; at any rate, I decided we would carry on for a bit, for the visibility might clear enough for us to risk a run inshore – if we could find the slightest indentation in the coast to give some shelter.

I knew from the chart that somewhere about eight miles ahead there was a kink in the coast at the Torre dell'Ovo – the Tower of Eggs. A small tongue of land curved out where the coast swung northward into a shallow bay – and it looked as though that torre held all our eggs, for there was no other shelter between us and it. But eight miles! That meant two hours. If the conditions remained static, it was possible; if they deteriorated more there was a grim choice left – to run ashore and say 'Goodbye' to *Lugworm* or try to ride it out, which I knew in my heart was probably, in our circumstances, the most risky course of all. You see, by running ashore, one does at least remain moving fast until the final moments when the boat either hits the beach in the surf, or rolls over very close inshore; to be swamped half a mile off a lee shore would mean either desperately clinging to a foundered boat (I had confidence that she would remain awash), or making a bid for it to swim ashore –

63

which would have meant almost certain drowning. Both of us, of course, had already donned our life-jackets, but you cannot really swim far in breaking seas, and not at all through surf, with its ever-present undertow just when, completely exhausted, you think you've gained the beach.

No! We would continue under engine, fighting to keep her buoyant.

I can recall vividly every minute of that next two hours. Evidently this was no small passing squall, for the wind continued undiminished and the seas steadily grew steeper. With the engine full throttle, and the wind helping on our port quarter, I reckoned we were making four knots and a bit, for occasionally *Lugworm* would take the reins and go for a long exciting surf down a sea's face. Again I was torn between two choices; to trail a rope and ease the engine revs so as to slow us down, allowing the seas to move quickly underneath – or to take that risk and speed on as fast as possible. We did the latter, but there was one final hurdle to be jumped.

Just to weather of that Tower of Omelettes, where the coast swung north a bit, was a shallow spit of rocks. According to our chart, it extended offshore for about three-quarters of a mile. I knew that the seas would be breaking even more steeply on this, yet the last thing I wanted in this situation was to get farther offshore: we were as close to the coast as I dared go, so that in the event of necessity we could run in within seconds. But there was really no choice – to seaward of these shallows we would have to go.

Little by little I eased her away from the shore, peering ahead desperately to try to make out some sign of the Tower and at last it appeared, a darker patch through the rain. 'Nearly there,' I encouraged B. who was doggedly bailing, for the deluge was filling the bilges. I knew that conditions close to leeward of that spit would be slightly better, for the shallow patch would have taken the brunt of the seas. It proved so, and luckily, since it was necessary to motor more across the seas while heading north into the lee of the point. But as we approached the sheltered basin, a grim picture presented itself. Quite unpredictably the swell was sweeping round the end of the spit to break with frightening strength right across the shallow entrance to the little bay. 'Lord!' I gasped to B. 'We just can't get in through that!'

Desperately we searched the coast farther on. About three cables beyond the bay a short line of rocks probed out from the shore, and close to them on their far side the sea was quite calm. It was also obviously very shallow, for even from our position we could see the green and brown of weeds and rocks under the surface. It seemed our only hope, for the small natural mole gave a good protection from the swell.

'We'll go in there and anchor close up under the rocks,' I bellowed at B., pointing. 'I daren't drive her actually ashore until we have had a look at the beach.' With rudder unshipped and the plate right up, we gingerly nosed round the end of the rocks, watching the seabed shallowing up, closer and closer, until finally *Lugworm* hit bottom hard once, twice, then surged in over a ridge into a small pool only a foot or two deep.

'Phew!' But I can tell you it's a wonderful feeling, to be suddenly safe after an experience like that. We stood in the boat and looked back out to sea. Under the black sky great rollers were thundering along, their tops lifting in a white frenzy of spray. 'Have we really escaped from that,' B. croaked. 'We're lucky,' I assured her, and in my heart sent out a silent message to John Watkinson, designer, and Brian Nicholls and John Elliot, builders, 'You'll never build a better boat, nor have more heartfelt thanks from any owner.'

But back to work. Our second anchor was laid out, and *Lugworm* positioned in the middle of the pool, as far away from all the rocks as possible, for even in here there was still an uneasy long surge. Satisfied that she was secure, we waded ashore to examine the beach. Both of us were soaked to the skin and very tired, for it had been exhausting work with nerves at full stretch. The whole beach was spattered with boulders and thick with dead weed, rolled and heaped into banks of black tarry muck. Provided we chose the spot carefully, it would be quite possible to bring the boat ashore here – which was preferable to remaining at anchor for still the storm showed no sign of abating.

Curiosity then took over and we staggered to the top of the beach. What sort of a coast was this that we had landed on? Over on the point, the square tower was obviously deserted, but in the other direction we could see a straggle of low bungalows, such as one might find at the small lidos which dotted the coast. Immediately inshore of us, at the end of its own short drive, was a two-storey house which also appeared to be empty. Not a soul was to be seen, and together we stood, palpitating gently like two frogs, then wandered over to a small coast road which ran from tower to village about a hundred yards inshore. We were standing near this in the lee of a small shed, sheltering from the wind and rain when there came a sudden and alarming silence. Gone was the howl of the storm – we were listening now only to the distant roar of the sea and the sudden loud patter of the rain. We looked at one another in disbelief.

'Maybe we shan't need to beach *Lugworm* after all,' B. remarked cautiously. But the sky remained that ghastly black, and off shore we could still see the fast scudding clouds rolling along. Even as we stood there, a lick of wind came swirling across the marram grass – straight out of the west.

We had passed through the middle of these local tempests before in Greece, but never had we experienced the suddenness or fury of that particular wind change. Within a minute we were fighting against a gale-force westerly that slammed at us with even greater fury than ever. We started to run back to the boat for she was now on a dead lee-shore, but even as I closed the beach, with B. staggering in pursuit, we saw her drive ashore, broach, lift to a sea and slew over on her side. The next sea filled her, and in horror I saw her lifted, half by the sheer force of the wind and half by the seas, up on top of a bank of tarry weed. Before I could reach her she had turned turtle. Thank God both masts were already down, or they would have been snapped like carrots. B. arrived, and together we frantically tried to shove *Lugworm's* bow into the seas and wind, for we were terrified that she would pound on a boulder and be stove in. But it is one thing to shift a heavy boat when she's the right way up and quite another to do it when she is upside down and half buried in great masses of weed. Each breaker – and they were increasing in size by the minute – brought a new morass of weed and sand spewing over her, swirling the sand away from under her as it receded again down the beach, until the poor boat seemed set on burying herself where she lay. Neither of us, exhausted as we were, could do a thing about it.

'Get those petrol cans clear,' I choked in B.'s ear. 'I'm going to try to get the outboard off her.' But the outboard was already buried deep in the filthy weed, its propeller sticking up helplessly, and fast as I scrabbled under the stern to get at the securing clamps another few hundredweights of water, weed and sand would come crashing over us. Desperately I searched the beach for a pole or baulk of wood with which, perhaps, the two of us might lever her back upright, and it was then I saw a figure running from the house towards us. It was a middle-aged man, his dark raincoat flapping wildly. 'Signore,' I roared, and then, because it was quite beyond me to say anything more, I merely pointed to the boat and idiotically repeated the word; what else was there to do? But there was no need for explanations; a backward Bedouin who'd never seen the sea would have grasped our immediate need. The three of us got our fingers under the shoreward gunwale – for that was the higher of the two – and heaved. With relief I saw *Lugworm* begin to tilt over. He was a powerful man, and while he and B. held her balanced, I knelt and got my haunches under the gunwale. I have a vivid recollection of Foogoo, entangled by his belly button in the netting under the side-deck festooned with weeds, as between the three of us we got the boat balanced precariously on one gunwale, holding her against the wall of wind.

'Careful!' I roared, terrified lest she should crash over and down the slope while there was no water there. 'Wait till I say "Now".' Mind you, I don't know who I thought I was talking to, for B. was beyond much in the way of strength, and our friend, up to his armpits in the scrimmage, had his ear jammed against the boat.

I watched till a sea came surging up the beach, then nodded to him and shoved. *Lugworm* tilted gently beyond the point of no return and crashed down, but her fall was softened by the upsurge of water, and as the next wave licked its way under her belly I shoved her head into the wind and tautened in on one of the anchor warps. She was a dreadful sight, half full of weed and sand, plastered with tar, and an indescribable tangle of rigging, sails and loose gear floating everywhere. But she was not holed.

An hour later, with the boat emptied of water and dragged farther up the beach (looking rather like a fly in a cobweb, so many warps had we rigged to hold her against the wind), we were able to pay more attention to our very real friend in need. Who was this man who had risked injury, ruined a suit and mackintosh and a good pair of shoes in the bargain to render help? He had saved *Lugworm* – there was no doubt of that.

'*Lei parla Inglese?*' we shrieked at him above the roar, but he merely waved a hand, indicating that it was little use trying to talk. He smiled, and pointed up to the house, where we could now see a lady standing on the verandah watching us.

'*Questa è la mia casa,*' he shouted, beckoning us to follow him.

Italo and Anna Maria Campa became our firm friends. We stayed in their house and were made most welcome for two nights while sorting out the mess aboard *Lugworm*. The tabernacle, though bent, could be straightened easily enough, and the bolts, fitted with larger washers were still usable. How the nuts and washers had drawn up through the wood without splitting it beyond repair is incredible, but it says a lot for the design and strength of the construction. Our spare set of rigging was fitted, and examination of the broken shroud revealed that the wire had parted at the soft eye which lies over the truck of the mainmast – a point I had deliberately protected with tubing against chafe, and this precaution was the very cause of my not detecting the fracture until it parted, for the wire had gradually weakened through constant flexing at the hard turn, completely hidden within the tube. One learns the hard way.

It was the morning of Friday 5th May that we finally pushed *Lugworm* back over that shallow rocky ridge, and with a farewell wave to our two new friends, set all sail for Taranto twenty miles up the coast.

*   *   *

'Fiume Lato, Bradano, Basento ... Fiume Agri, Sinni, Trionto ... Fiume Neto.' As each river name rolled off B.'s tongue, her small finger stabbed down the coastline on our chart which was spread across a flat stone balustrade on Taranto's waterfront. 'That's seven; we ought to find shelter in one, at least.' Above us a cloud of moths mobbed the yellow lamp-glass half hidden in the branches of a dusty orange tree which helped keep at bay the strident clamour of traffic in the wide boulevard beyond. Between us and the dark Mare Piccolo – Taranto's 'Little Sea' – the busy quays stretched as far as eye could follow.

Scores of fishing craft, their flared bows gaily painted and numbered, were drifting with engines quietly throbbing or shoving impatiently alongside the tightly packed quays, shouldering their way in amid raucous but good natured banter from the crews. Above the hubbub an occasional deep-throated roar of a powerful diesel would assert itself, commanding brief attention as, with lifting bow-wave, a boat shook free of the congestion to sweep into the canal out beneath towering battlements of the old fortress, into the blackness of the Mare Grande.

Behind and above it all rose the impressive squalor of the old city, mellow in the dark night like a backcloth painted on the sky to enhance the bustling activity of the waterfront, where once again her vast fishing fleet was preparing for sea. It was a vital and noisy scene. A hundred yards along the quayside two rival gangs of youngsters were waging full-scale war. Stones flying and fists flailing, the battle surged back and forth across the balustrade, in among the orange trees and into the road, then back again over the busy quay until a stone, wide of its mark, brought a sudden explosion of anger from a tight-knit group of fishermen. As one, the group surged towards the battle area; a shrill cry of warning and, with a last fling, the opposing warriors scattered before the common enemy, their retreat sounded by falling glass splinters from yet another conquered lamp standard. Uneasy truce.

But this evening one sensed another focal point of interest; a new topic was under discussion other than the prices their catch might fetch or the weather conditions out there in the Gulf. Who were these two foreigners in their small black boat with the finely carved teak quarter badges? Where had they appeared from, and what were they doing down there at the end of the quay in the hubbub of this old port? She was no working boat, that was obvious, for though small she carried herself with the airs of a yacht and yet ... why then was she not anchored off the elegant yacht club out there in the Mare Grande, her owners knocking back their Martinis and Camparis under the awnings? There was mystery here. In the line of her sheer and the flare of her bow, the boat had a marked similarity to their own rugged fishing craft; and the two sitting up there on the balustrade studying the chart – English, eh? They neither of them looked much like the dandy yachting folk one sometimes sells fish to at exorbitant prices out there in the Gulf. Too lean and brown and wiry ... can't he afford shoes then? There are sly grins. *'Zuanne,'* shouts a voice, *'Tuo cuggino cha la tua Nana Inglese,'* – roars of laughter – *'Vai a vedere cosa Fanno.'*

'It seems to me,' said B. poring over the chart, 'that the Basento is our likeliest first attempt at a river. It's twenty miles as the crow flies clipping straight across the top of the Gulf; but all these rivers are mighty shallow off the mouth – under a fathom and sandy bottom. It's ...'

'Engleeesh?' came the cheery call. A swarthy dark haired fisherman was filling a bucket from the tap adjacent. 'I spek Engleesh, yes.'

'*Amico!*' I responded, throwing out my arms as to a friend in need, '*Parla lei Inglese?* We need your help with local knowledge, can you spare a moment?' His face fell, the smile faded and a look of blank incomprehension took its place. From behind him, a roar of laughter arose from the nearest group around the boats.

'*No, Signore, io non parlo Inglese,*' came the shamefaced reply, but then the teeth flashed again. '*Parla Italiano lei?*'

'*Poco, poco,*' B. answered, but her reply was drowned in ribald comments from his watching companions.

'*Itte sese fattende insarasa, Zuanne, ses-giai proponende a sa brunda, eh! E tue un omini sposadu. Torra ai noghe e narrame itte ase iscrobettu faiddende su Inglesu chi faeddas tue … la finisi de le faghere sos ogos drucches su maridu este arribbende. Impizzade de sa pisca tua Zuanne … Mi la presentasa, seu mannu abbastanza.*'

Our friend seemed embarrassed. I could guess something of the nature of the shouted conversations taking place and, keen to widen the tenuous contact which had been made, beckoned him over at the same time pointing to our chart. My gesture brought some twenty of his inquisitive companions strolling across as well. We were surrounded by a grinning horde of black-browed, brown skinned fisherfolk, and one of them pointing to my bare feet broke into voluble Italian. To a clamour of approval he started removing his rubber thighboots intending, I feared, to give them to me.

'*Amici, amici,*' I bellowed above the hubbub, in my atrocious Italian, grinning more broadly than perhaps I felt. '*Noi siamo Inglesi … barca mia,*' and I pointed to *Lugworm*. '*Noi andiamo in lnghilterra in barca. Noi …*' I got no further. A stunned silence had fallen on the crowd. From along the quay yet more of their companions were joining us. One and all they turned and looked at *Lugworm*, then pandemonium broke out.

72

'Ses navighende subra e custu finzasa a Inghilterra! Suba e custu ... Ma ses maccu ... Passas mare malu subra e custu.' The amazement was obvious.

'Noi arrivamo de la Grecia,' I explained. 'We come from Greece and we are sailing home to England,' and jumping off the wall I clasped two of them by the arm, leading them to the edge of the quay. *'Vengano,'* I invited, and jumped aboard, beckoning them to follow. Four heavy feet dropped on *Lugworm's* after deck and amid ribald comment she heeled dangerously over from the quay, where the large crowd had gathered to watch. I opened the lockers, showed how our clothes and food stowed, how we cooked, where the clock and the barometer stowed and how the rudder shipped down the trunking, for this latter always caused a good deal of interest in Greece, being quite unusual. *'Plastica?'* queried a voice from on shore. *'No ... legno compensato marino ... Tutto in legno compensato marino, niente plastica.'* They showed tremendous interest, but the whole object of my exercise was not yet accomplished. I needed to show we were friends, as good as they were, unafraid, and that we trusted them; perhaps that was now clear. So what about us seeing over their boats, eh?

I was very keen to examine these boats, for I knew something of their history. They represent the end of a continuous line of evolution lasting more than 2,600 years. Their owners, these 'Tarantines', were descendants from an ancient stock who originally left Greece under the stigma of 'Spartan Bastards'. Illegitimate children of Greek soldiers, tired of being away from home during the long wars of that period, the 'Parthenoi' as they were then known, rebelled at their low social standing and left Sparta to become independent and found their own colony here in Southern Italy. As is so often the case with new mixed blood the stock was virile and intelligent. 'Taras,' as the port was then known, rapidly became one of the richest and most powerful cities of the ancient Magna Graecia, proud in her prime to muster an army of some thirty thousand infantry, as well as the famous Tarantine Cavalry. Now we were sharing their famous 'Little Sea' and proposed exploring their fascinating coastline where even today very few pleasure craft penetrate. We were entirely in their hands, and they were good hands to be in, if friendly, for none knew better than they every contour of this desolate coast ahead.

It is surprising how much can be conveyed despite language barriers, when a common interest is shared. I was shown over many craft there under the lamps of the quayside, and after accepting one gift of a fine little squid, had difficulty in refusing more, but somehow managed to convey that there was one very real way in which they could help us: to tell us which, if any, of the rivers between here and Cape Spartivento we might possibly enter.

Back under the lamp again, with the chart spread over the wide balustrade and dividers at the ready, we systematically eliminated one river after another.

'Lato?' I would stab at the river on the chart. 'Possibile di entrando?' A dozen opinions were voiced: on balance it was 'No' – and Bradano? Yes, that was possible for your little boat, perhaps, but shallow. Basento? So-so, shoulders were shrugged, perhaps, perhaps not. There had been much rain inland, it would make a strong current and shifting sandbanks. Hands were swung to indicate overfalls and current at the mouth ... pericoloso! And Fiume Agri ... ah, yes perhaps, but enter from the north side of the mouth, eh Pietro? Much discussion ... but yes, Agri could be entered ... and so it went on, with B. making notes, and then general discussion and interest returned once more to *Lugworm*. I showed them a drawing of the dinghy with

74

centreplate lowered and rudder shipped, to give an idea of the draught when sailing. There was much concern – general advice was offered; we must beware, with the wind off the land it was good, but if the winds came from the south – take care! We already knew this, but it was good to hear confirmation. Sirocco! Heads were wagged; altogether it was quite clear that we were mad, but interestingly so.

*   *   *

And now Taranto's extensive western mole is far behind us, like a thin grey thread drawn delicately along the horizon. As we watch, it grows more tenuous, breaks, and finally disappears altogether leaving only a blinding white and faintly curving coast which dances in the heat ahead and astern until this too merges into the far-off pearl of sea and sky. Low hillocks of marram grass flank the beach, backed here and there by scrub tamarisk and odd clumps of small windblasted pines. For close on two hundred and fifty miles ahead our chart shows no harbour save Crotone which lies half that distance away. It is a magnificent morning with just the ghost of a south westerly breeze pressing *Lugworm* along, and no other boat in sight; the seemingly endless shore and the sea and the sky are ours alone.

Conversation wanes. We laze in the brilliant sun and watch the beach, some two cables away, drift silently past. A torre, ethereal, and seemingly transparent like a dream castle quivers and flows into the scene ahead. We watch as it solidifies, assumes the proportions proper to an earthbound thing of solid stone, and gazes with empty eyes out to the horizon, quite oblivious of our tiny boat, as though its soul were withdrawn and far away, dreaming of ancient days when it pulsed with urgent warning of approaching fleets. We watch as it slowly dissolves again astern, the only changing object in a never changing shore, and the sun grows ever hotter. Already the two of us are tanned to match our teak gunwales. B. has taken to wearing her sampan hat, a straw circular creation about three feet in diameter. I wear nothing, since it's much better for the constant cooling flops over the side; and then there is the flask of dry white wine, and a dish of olives to idle away the noonday torpor; can you imagine anything nearer to Paradise on earth?

Not if you're me, you can't.

"Do you know,' I say after an hour or so of soporific content, and more to ensure that B. hasn't passed out from sunstroke than from any urgent wish to break the silence. 'Do you know that at this moment there are millions of benighted humans ferreting away in offices in the warrens of vast metropolis,' I pride myself on my plurals, 'Some of them may even glance occasionally at the window – if there is a window, but what need of a window when there are tubes of synthetic neon blazing down on their sickly pallor from the ceiling? Would you not rather be there?' I ask her provocatively.

'Oh,' she muses, dangling a long leg overboard and clasping her hands over the crown of that ridiculous hat, which makes it look like an inverted Elizabethan flower basket, 'there are lots of jobs I would rather be doing than that, like driving a tube train on the Circle Line, or operating a lift in one of those large department stores.'

'Well, there's blessed little fear of that,' I comment. 'Both those occupations require a built-in sense of feeling and expertise. Even with long training I doubt they'd put you in charge.' One of her delightfully irritating ineptitudes is a total inability to push the right knob, or turn a dial the right way at first attempt, and often even a second attempt. This has nothing to do with intelligence – she can sail rings round me when it comes to a game of chess or a crossword puzzle, but give her anything remotely electrical or mechanical and you might as well be ready to dial 999.

This taunt provokes nothing but a prolonged and deserved silence, charged with faint dudgeon. Ashore, a small domed grey concrete gunpost, its slit eyes cocked skywards, sags on the undercut edge of the shingle, forlorn monument to man's eternal inhumanity.

'Have an olive, cuckoo.'

Silence.

There is a distant low rumble of thunder somewhere up there in the hills of Basilicata to the north. The hat jerks upright.

'Yes … well …' I comment. Both of us are thinking the same thought. This, more or less, is how it all began back there at the Tower of Eggs. The wind is dying; indeed, now one thinks of it, *Lugworm* too is almost asleep, her three tan sails idly collapsing with ennui. We study the chart again but there isn't a kink worth looking at until it cuts off just south of Cape Spulico and that's forty miles away. 'We could start the engine, but it seems a terrible waste of fuel at sixty pence a gallon,' I suggest. But B. is looking ahead through the glasses.

'There's something dark sticking out from shore ahead there. Looks like a pier, but it may be anything in the mirage … take a look.'

Sure enough, a dancing line of dark probes out from the beach just on the edge of visibility. We start the engine and stow the sails, and soon it is clear that a low concrete mole has been constructed but there is nothing to suggest why; not a house or tower or any sign of habitation. As we close its seaward end another parallel mole comes into view about fifty yards beyond. They both bury themselves into the sand of the beach. *Lugworm* noses in between the two, where the slight swell that is running fails to penetrate, and we ground gently, taking the anchor up the sand. Together we walk up the hot sand, half afraid to talk lest the sound disturb the absolute torpid silence. Over the ridge of the beach a green shallow pool probes back into luxuriant foliage. Reeds quiver as a kingfisher darts away in surprise. Trees, thick and green, crowd the banks, as though overbalancing in their haste to drink the fresh water.

As we stand looking across the lagoon a faint rumble makes itself felt, but this is not thunder; it is continuous and gaining volume every second. 'Of course,' B. says, 'the railway,' and we sit to await the passing of the train. It thunders towards us, quite invisible somewhere back there in the trees, roars by in a crescendo of sound, then just as quickly dies away somewhere beyond, leaving an even more profound silence. But the sky is turning that familiar purple, as though suffocating with its own heat, and we return to *Lugworm*, mooring her securely with a bow anchor out seaward and a couple of stern warps to prevent her ranging, then rig the tent for there seems little point in motoring on. It is just gone midday and there is no breath of wind. What is more, this freshwater lagoon intrigues us, for if it is the end of a river, either it is a river with no water in its upper reaches or, if there is water flowing in, it must be escaping into the sea by slowly permeating through the sand of the beach itself, for there is no mouth. The latter bodes ill for our hopes of getting into the rivers for night shelter, but this is a good opportunity for exploration; these concrete moles, evidently built during the war for some military purpose, provide a useful shelter should the sea turn wild overnight.

That evening we walked deep back inland through stunted pine woods following a beaten track beside the river whose green water seemed to be quite still though not stagnant, which suggested that in fact there was a slight flow. The bridge carrying the railway appeared within a quarter of a mile inland, and beyond that a long straight road running parallel with no sign of traffic. Here the woods ended and the whole flat land was cultivated for some distance either side the water, and after a while the river seemed to have been canalised, its banks becoming straight and obviously dug out as an irrigation channel.

It was at some forgotten hour of the night that an alien sound awoke me. A steady and unaccountable hiss grew in strength, and across the white canvas of the tent a moving shadow crept, thrown by the approach of a powerful light. The brilliance increased until inside the boat was like daylight.

B. sat up with a startled 'Whatever … ?' and I checked that my plastic toy revolver was to hand, for while in Greece we had been warned that along this lonely stretch of coast the local 'banditi' might make themselves a nuisance. I had bought the toy gun in case of such emergency. But a soft call, *'Amico … amico …'* put my fears to rest. Blinded by the light, I poked my head out of the open end of the tent, to see a small fishing boat with its two pressure lamps approaching. The grinning face of Zuanne shone in the lights and as his companion 'back watered' with his oars a great wet squid was slapped down on to our after deck.

'Grazie, amico. .. molto grazie,' I called to him, and watched as they pulled back past the mole ends, to gradually diminish until their light joined that of the stars, balanced there over the horizon. It was a kindness and good to know they were evidently keeping a friendly watch on our activities.

We stayed in that unnamed river mouth all next day, and saw not a soul. No breath of wind stirred the sea's face, and the weather remained sultry and treacherous, the sky turning horribly black at early evening. But the following morning – the 9th May – we were off early before a light land breeze. Alas, within the hour the breeze failed, and reluctantly the engine had once more to come to the rescue.

In the late forenoon it was evident that we were approaching the mouth of the Bradano river, for we noticed the water close inshore turning to a muddy brown, with a quite clear demarcation line between it and the clear blue of the sea. Ahead we could see what appeared to be a low line of tamarisk and other small trees growing out into the sea. Sailing within yards of the shore as we were, this 'bulge' of land at the mouth of the larger rivers was most pronounced. It is caused by the gradual deposit of silt brought down with the river water. This builds up a projection out into the sea, and on this fertile bulge trees take root. From the chart it is scarcely detectable, but when viewed along the line of the shore, due to the low-lying nature of the bulge and the heightening affect of the mirage on the trees, it gives the peculiar appearance from afar as of tall trees actually growing out of the sea. As we approached these river mouths, it was impossible to detect depth by eye since the water always became too thick with mud or sand and always this brown fresh water crept up along the coastline to meet us before we arrived, thus revealing a slight surface drift in a northerly direction.

The Bradano river was one of those stated by our friends in Taranto to be navigable, so in view of the lack of wind we decided to call it a day and try to enter: but it was not so easy. To start with there was a strong outflow: about two to three knots. As always happens when a swell meets a flow of water running in contrary direction the height of the swell rapidly increased and the wave-length decreased. This resulted in slight surf some distance off the entrance, but it was a calm day and presented little hazard so with rudder unshipped and the centreplate up, we gingerly nosed under power towards the river mouth. Considering the quantity of muddy water drifting up the coast this mouth was surprisingly small – not more than a hundred yards across at most I would guess. B. stationed herself at the bow with an oar which she used as a sounding pole, while I perched on the stern at the outboard, ready to lift the propeller at a second's warning, for it was clear from the behaviour of the water there was a shallow bar across the entrance. Round my waist I had a warp made fast, its other end leading forward clear of the shroud and fast to the foredeck cleat. This was a precaution in case I had to jump overboard. The problem as we saw it was that of hitting bottom right in the mouth where the current was strongest. In this event the engine could not be used for fear of damaging the propeller, hence the possible need for me to jump overboard and tow *Lugworm* across the bar into the quiet water behind. To lose power at the moment of crossing the bar would simply result in our being drifted out to sea again.

In the Bradano entrance this proved unnecessary, for the minimum sounding gave three feet, and although the breakers were popping us about a bit we got in without trouble.

It was fun entering that first river, and gave valuable clues for use on future occasions. One learns to sense the deeper channels by the appearance of the surface and soon we found the hidden snags. For instance, when approaching the mouth it was necessary to aim for that small area where the swell from seaward broke least. This may sound obvious, but in fact it can be the most hazardous point, for by virtue of the fact that it indicates the deeper channel it also ensures that when and if the swell does break therein, it will be a real thumper. Often we would lie off a mouth, watching the wave patterns for half an hour and more before deciding exactly where and when the least risky approach might be made. Remember that a capsize or foundering in the entrance would result in our being immediately swept back into and through the breakers which in such a situation, could prove very dangerous.

But once inside the mouth, the transition from blinding blue sea and white beaches to dark green water and the shade of overhanging trees and tall reeds was like a long cool drink to a thirsty man. We would motor up slowly against the current, exploring the river for a mile or two with a view to a good night berth. Let the storms arrive; once we were inside the mouth we knew there was no danger, and this was our constant concern along this shallow harbourless coast. In the early days we would choose to sleep ashore on some grassy patch perhaps amongst the scrub bushes, but we soon found that the farther away from the sea the more the gnats and other biting insects made life difficult. Subsequently, in rivers up the western seaboard of Italy we would always moor as close to the entrance as possible, anchoring the boat against the sandy banks near to the sea and clear of trees, for this reduced trouble from winged nippers. My own hide seems to be immune from the pests, but poor B. was obviously a repast worth flying miles to savour.

They were wonderful days, and we shall always remember this instep of Italy as being one of the most adventurous and carefree parts of our cruise home for we are by nature 'loners', far preferring the solitude of country to the gregariousness and noise of towns and harbours. You may guess that marinas with their barrack-like parking slots are anathema to us.

The evenings were spent beachcombing for drift wood for the night fire, wandering miles along the shore, stretching our legs after a day in the boat, smelling all those hidden scents of the land which are denied one at sea. We came close to that sense of adventure which must have attended the original explorers of the world, for although we had a chart of the coast, we never knew what the terrain just inshore of the beach would provide. In fact, my impression of this stretch of the coast is of scrub tamarisk and tall grasses swept back like hair, bleached and combed by the salty winter gales, while that area immediately around the river mouths would bear every sign of being inundated with fast flowing water. Although parched and dry now, the boles of the trees were wrapped around up to three feet above their bases with dead reeds, grasses and the branches of smaller trees where the flood waters of winter had left them.

We would light a wood fire at the top of the beach, well away from the dry scrub behind, and cook our evening meal as the light faded. The smoke would keep the insects at bay, and afterwards in the darkness our flickering circle of light would be like a small oasis far away from the noise and stresses of our modern world. Sometimes, behind us in the undergrowth or perhaps among the pine forests, we would hear a herd of wandering water buffalo, or the sudden stamp of a horse's hoof, but very seldom did we see any living thing. The beaches were thick with bleached driftwood, and there was never any shortage of fuel.

But the really tricky part of this lonely coast was yet to be tackled. We had now rounded the top of the Gulf and were working southward where the coast is different in character to the northern shores. The hills of Calabria down towards the toe crowd to the edge of the sea, grooved by vast 'torrentes' – mountain rivers – which hold cataracts of water only during the rain periods of autumn and winter. Their dried-up beds, strewn with boulders that have been washed down by the force of the torrent, look like grey wounds down the green face of the mountains, and the shore tends to be of shingle and boulders rather than sand.

It was shortly after leaving the Fiume Agri on 12th May that we anchored just north of Cape Spulico, close ashore to miss a nasty swell and sea which was bowling up before a brisk heading south-west wind. I was undecided at midday whether to leave this small lee and tackle the next stretch of coast, for I was doubtful whether we would manage to enter either the Straface or Seraceno rivers with the amount of swell which was running. In the event the wind eased somewhat by 1600 and since our chart indicated (it was a mere suggestion of a line) that there might be a small protective mole off the coastal town of Trebisacce eight miles south of the Cape, we took the risk and started a quick nip under power into the teeth of the wind. It proved to be a mistake, for instead of dying, as we had expected, with the evening, the wind freshened. Indeed, so strong did it become that we unshipped the mizzen and lowered the mainmast in an effort to reduce windage and ease the burden on our tiny outboard. To make matters worse the wind had taken a slant southward which, though not allowing us to sail along the coast without the need to tack frequently, had made it a lee shore. By 1730 we could see the tiny mole ahead, but to our dismay it turned out to be a pier, mounted on pylons which gave no protection whatever from the swell and sea which was rolling up the coast. Two choices were open to us: we could either turn tail and sail back round Cape Spulico, or we could beach the boat at Trebisacce. The beach here was of medium sized pebbles, but steep.

Our approach, however, had not gone unnoticed by the small town. As we closed the pier a crowd of interested fisher-folk collected. Their own boats were already drawn up high on the beach, and when one of them – a large powerful man in thigh-boots – waved to us to go ashore the decision was made. We anchored a few yards off the beach, outside the line of breakers, and rigged the rope girdle attaching the lanyard for rigging the tackle. This was observed with great interest by those on shore, who had been joined by many of the townsfolk. I stood in the stern and pointed to the place I had selected to run ashore. Instantly the fishermen lined the beach, beckoning us in. With B. easing out on the bow anchor I put the engine full astern, then just as we entered the danger area of the breakers lifted the unit and locked it up. Willing hands rushed into the sea. I threw them the sternrope and so expert were these folk at hauling boats out of surf that B. and I were still in *Lugworm* as thirty or so powerful arms lifted and carried her bodily up the shingle.

We did not know it then, but this was to be our billet for seven days as the swell increased, breaking farther and farther up the shingle banks and quite precluding any thought of launching. In company with the fishing boats, *Lugworm* was drawn progressively farther and farther back up the beach as each day brought worse seas, and we began to wonder whether in the end we would not have to be hauled right across the coast road. They were a grand lot, those fishermen. We came to know many of them well, and as in all these seaside communities found that one of the older men was a sort of 'father of the beach'. Gaitano, or 'Poppa' as we came to endearingly refer to him, would come down each morning to enquire after our welfare. If anything needed doing, he it was who would organise it, such as dragging the boat farther away from the encroaching surge, arranging a free supply of drinking water from the communal fishermen's store – and seeing that we were informed of any arrival of fresh fish from down the coast, for at the moment the entire fleet of Trebisacce, with *Lugworm*, was pinned on shore by this weather.

We walked scores of miles back up the hills into the small hilltop towns, now largely deserted by the youngsters who preferred to move to the coast where more money was to be made.

Always we were happy that *Lugworm* was in safe hands. The natural courtesy of these folk would eliminate any embarrassments due to the lack of privacy aboard. No one would approach in the mornings until one of us had shown a head through the after tent flap; thereafter there would be the welcome greetings, a survey of the weather, and various forecasts. As the days went by, we began to feel one of the community, and evidently the word was spreading about these two oddities in their remarkable boat who were sailing to England. Much advice was offered, with repeated warnings to beware of such and such a community farther down towards the toe, for these were 'bad men' – 'banditi' who might steal from us. It was the same wherever we made contact with these small shore towns – always we were warned against the inhabitants of the next town down the coast; always we found them wholly delightful, considerate and helpful. It is human nature, after all, and the same this world over.

We learned much of their methods of fishing while shore-bound at Trebisacce. One day, while walking along the beach about five miles to the north we came across a figure running towards us just above the waterline. He was towing a long line, some three hundred feet of it, and must have run a full mile as we watched. Suddenly we saw him stop, anchor the inboard end of the line with a boulder and proceed to haul in slowly. There were about thirty hooks with spinners attached at ten foot intervals, and we helped him land a whacking big fish – some four feet in length of a type we could not identify. What interested us was the method of keeping the line out in deep water. Attached to the outboard end was a sort of orange box without top or bottom made in the shape of a paravane so that it constantly pulled away from the point of tow. He called it a 'carillo', and it gave us ideas for when we arrived back here at home in our own estuary for fishing during the winter when *Lugworm* is laid up.

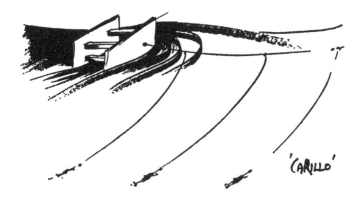

The Trebisacce fishermen operated a small fleet of boats about eighteen feet in length, strongly built and some of them with long sweeps, others with outboard motors. All the boats were 'double enders' so a small transom had to be rigged on which the outboard might be housed. The night before we left they launched the boats just after dark, each with its powerful pressure lamp lit over the stern, and it was fascinating to see them being hauled down the beach, the outboard already running before they hit the water, ready to take them instantly clear of the breakers. On one or two occasions the boats without outboards – those with oars alone – were knocked back by the still considerable swell before the oars could get sufficient grip to take take them clear into deep water. It was great fun, undertaken with a tremendous sense of humour and comradeship, not without sarcastic banter when things went wrong and a boat ended up broadside on shore with half its crew up to their waists in the breakers.

We were both sad and glad to get launched again on the 20th May early in the morning, all our friends giving us a welcome shove down the beach. The residual swell from the recent bad weather was still causing a lot of white water along the shore, but as we worked south past Fiume Crati the coast began to swing eastward, enabling us to free off somewhat before the south-west wind, and giving us a spanking sail along to the Fiume Trionto, the small and shallow entrance of which we entered at 1430, just west of the lighthouse on the Cape. We were rounding Alice Point and heading due south towards Crotone in the early afternoon of the following day, and put into the Fiume Neto eight miles north of Crotone that evening.

I shall remember that entry. We stood off and watched the wave patterns off the river mouth for a while, the wind being light from the south, enabling us to make the entry under sail. But alas things did not go so well this time. Of course the rudder had to be unshipped, and steering was effected with an oar through the stern rowlock, but there was a strong outflow and lumpy overfalls on the shallow bar. *Lugworm* hit the bottom solidly, coming to a halt just as a breaker hit her stern. I jumped out, attached by the lanyard to her bow, and was pulling against the current while B. steered. But that current was shifting the sand under my feet, and if I stood in one place for more than a second or so found that I was gradually sinking lower and lower into the riverbed. Finally, I hit quicksand, sinking down to my waist when the strong current immediately carried me and the boat back into and through the breakers again. Oh, it was tremendous fun, and we made it on the second attempt, by the simple expedient of using the engine, but not before losing a lot of paint off the propeller blades, the tips of which were bright metal from the sanding-down they received. Last month while completely stripping down the engine here at home, I found a great deal of sand inside the cooling water system, much of it I'm sure, came from the River Neto and brought back memories.

Crotone was hovering just over the horizon to the south. We sailed from Neto next day – an exciting exit through large breakers – and headed under all sail before a brisk north westerly which was building up the seas off the harbour entrance. By the time we made the entrance we were surfing more than sailing, skidding down the large waves which were beginning to break some half mile from the harbour mole. It was good to get into the shelter of the Porto Nuovo, the new north harbour, but we found it too commercial for our liking, and later that evening, when the wind and seas had eased, motored round to the Porto Vecchio, the quieter old south harbour.

Most of the small coastal villages were little more than fishing settlements in this area, often poverty stricken and squalid. Many of the houses, shanty-built on the beaches, were dilapidated and ruined. This may have been due to earthquake tremors or merely to the undermining of the foundations due to their proximity to the sea, for they appeared to be erected on sand. There were no harbours, the boats being drawn up the beaches, and as we approached often the inhabitants would run to the water's edge and imperiously wave us in. But unless we needed provisions we kept our distance. One pleasant surprise; having rounded Cape Colonne and Cape Rizzuto we came across a newly constructed port at Marina di Catanzaro, spending a pleasant evening there.

But we were now in the heart of the infamous 'Gulf of Squalls' and the sooner we could get down south and round that big toe the better. In the event it turned out to be easier than we expected. We sailed from Catanzaro early on the 24th May, but before noon the wind fell away light. Under the outboard we pressed on down to the toe, rounding Cape Spartivento at midnight. It was fascinating taking compass bearings on the lights of hilltop villages. A flying fish came aboard with a great clatter, but apart from that the calm night passed uneventfully. Dawn, however, brought a rising north wind which found us beating wetly up round Capo dell'Armi to drop anchor in the lee of the Bay of San Gregorio just south of Reggio at 0600 on Thursday 25th May.

Ahead lay the Straits of Messina.

CHAPTER III

Sicily and the Aeolian Islands

IN ITS STRUGGLE FOR SURVIVAL the swordfish, poor innocent, has fallen into the trap of adopting inflexible habits. About the end of February each year this fish's thoughts lightly turn to love and having chosen a mate the couple stay together with utmost fidelity. Moreover, they then leave the colder northern waters and swim south to honeymoon in warmer areas. From early June they may be found in the Straits of Messina lazing around just beneath the surface. One more mistake they have made is in being very good to eat.

Long before Christ, the predator Man had detected these fatal flaws in their pattern of behaviour. But the swordfish is one of the fastest moving creatures of the sea. Sensitive and alert, it is known to take violent alarm at the slightest alien vibration of water. It was observed, however, that this intelligent creature had learned to a fine point exactly how near a stealthily approaching boat might close before the need to take flight. By mounting a pole in the boat up which a lookout – called a *guadiano* – might climb, the fish could be seen some distance off. By further fixing a stout plank over the bow of the boat a skilled and agile harpoonist called the *allanzatore* could, with luck, strike a split second before the fish's alarm system said 'flee'.

With the march of progress in the form of steel girders and high tensile rigging wire, the gap in time between 'harpoon strike' and 'flight alarm' has been extended and today, if you are

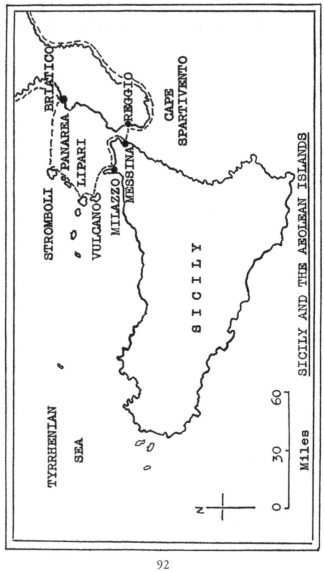

SICILY AND THE AEOLEAN ISLANDS

lucky enough to be in the Straits of Messina you will in summer see the swordfish boats, or *ontri* as they are called, erratical-
ly probing about with the most incredible lattice girder masts
some sixty feet high at the very top of which is perched the
guadiano who, I'm told, now communicates with the helms-
man below by a sophisticated intercom system of microphone
and earphones, all aimed at maintaining the utmost possible
silence.

Out over the bow is another slender lattice of equal length,
stayed to the top of the mast like some brain child of Emmet's,
and at the tip of this you will see the allanzatore with his two-
pronged harpoon. Watch carefully through binoculars and you
may well see this man very smoothly raise his *triccia*, as the
weapon is called, taking care not to jerk or make any sound,
then spear downward with tremendous power and accuracy.
More often than not, once this strike has been made the water
below will erupt in violent protest as the impaled fish fights to
free itself of the horribly barbed spear. Its mate likewise will frequently swim frantically round in desperation, trying to find
some cause of the companion's anguish, itself thus often falling
prey to a second harpoon. Thereafter the ever-weakening fish
will be 'played' on the end of the stout line which is attached to
the harpoon, finally to be brought alongside and hauled aboard
the ontri. When you consider that an average sized swordfish
may weigh around one hundred and ten pounds – sometimes
much more – you will appreciate that this whole recovery
process is not easily undertaken, particularly if the fish has not
suffered a seriously disabling strike.

Like most hunting, it is all a deplorable and beastly occupa-
tion but, as we all have to learn, such unnatural human con-
cepts as morality bed ill with natural human appetite, and when
like me you sit down to an exquisite swordfish steak, grilled in

olive oil with a liberal sprinkling of lemon juice, oregano and finely chopped mint, Satan, no doubt, has a good belly laugh.

We sailed from San Gregorio fully provisioned and watered, beating against a brisk north wind and a southerly set of current, using the coastal indentations so far as possible to gain to windward up the narrow Straits until abeam of Reggio, then reached across to the Sicilian shore, picking up a useful northerly set of tide which helped us up past Messina where we anchored for the night close under a palpitating funfair on Punta Paradiso.

On looking back, this passage through the Strait marked a distinct change in the ambience of our cruise. It were as though we had passed through a doorway into another room; a room where Man had again taken over Nature, and was solidly in charge. Islands and lonely places there were in abundance on the rest of the trip, but always Nature had been tamed, the land cultivated, the sea used, the rivers fished, bridged and boated upon; unlike those desolate untamed stretches of Italy's instep.

'The last time I crossed this Strait,' I remarked to B., gazing up at the white tipped peak of Etna smoking far away in Sicily, 'was in a Landing Craft in 1943. We ferried George Formby and his wife Beryl, complete with piano and an ENSA group across to a delightful little marble jetty at Reggio which has now disappeared. The war stopped while we unloaded the damned piano; funny how you remember the inconsequential things.'

I looked north to where the colossal pylons elegantly draped their high power cables across from Italy to Sicily. 'And I can tell you why it was that Scylla and Charybdis, those two horrific whirlpools, stopped tormenting sailors in the narrow mouth up there, though nobody else knows it. We dropped a bronze offering in the form of a valuable propeller blade; it was a great sacrifice too – the ship nearly fell to bits with the vibration, and it put us in dry dock for a week. But it was evidently appreciated.'

Indeed, it was strange looking into the harbour of Messina and remembering how it had appeared thirty years before. The figure of Christ was still perched up there on the column at the mole end, but gone were the deserted quays, the ruined silent grey cadavers of the badly bombed town. Gone was the rusty and burnt-out shell of an enormous cruise liner, heeled over on her side on the beach just outside the harbour, her funnel lapping the waterline. I looked across to the hills of Calabria in Italy: tonight there would be no red glow of forest fires up there, as there were in 1943. No fat grey shape of a Monitor would glide silently down the Straits, her massive long range guns ready to pump tons of high explosive into enemy positions, softening up the interior after consolidation on the invasion beaches.

Ashore the hurdy-gurdies of the funfair blazed into the night, their clarion music echoing across the Strait. Lean hydrofoils, like angry wasps, darted from the harbour, bound for Reggio. Ferries lobbed past, their wakes making *Lugworm* roll mightily all night, and on the coast road the roar of traffic with its urgent horns proclaimed the tenacity and resurgence of human spirit.

We motored beneath the pylon wires in a dead flat calm the following morning within feet of the shore to escape the tremendous southerly flow, turned west to skirt along the north Sicilian shore, and rounded Cape Peloro at 1000. The Ionian lay behind us. Ahead was the five hundred odd miles of Italy's Tyrrhenian seaboard and we knew that up there the summer winds prevailed light from the north west, which boded ill for our sailing. But first, there were those enchanting Aeolian Islands dotted about out there off the north coast of Sicily; it was impossible to look at a chart and by-pass them, but in the event it turned out a hard battle to make any westing along that north shore. It was a fascinating area, long sandy beaches being backed with low hills behind, and I remember the sea was thick with pumice chips and there was, alas, a lot of tar on the beaches.

Before noon the wind had freshened into a dead header and clear of Cape Rasocolmo was knocking up a nasty wetting sea. We put into the lee of the Cape and anchored close to the beach, up which a long surge was beginning to run. Shortly after our arrival four stalwart brown Sicilians hove up in a fishing boat which they promptly ran ashore, and hauled up high and dry on a small sled attached to a hand windlass.

It was pretty obvious we weren't going to make Milazzo in the lee of the promontory fifteen miles ahead under sail that day and the opportunity was too good to miss. I bellowed at them, pointing to *Lugworm* and the sled. Within minutes we were high and dry up the splendid sandy beach, alongside the other craft. It was always like that, everybody was only too willing to help.

* * *

There are times, I suspect, when B. is convinced I'm mad. This is one of them. You had better know that when the hours drag – and they've been dragging on this gritty beach under Rasocolmo for too long, with a high wind and sand in our molars – I'm given to standing on my head. This in itself is not particularly odd; I know a lot of intelligent people who do it and a lot of politicians who ought to. It flushes the brain, keeps the scalp healthy, nourishes the roots of the hair, and relieves the circulatory valves. It also presents the world in a different light, which often helps.

Ken Duxbury, the Author

'B', the Crew

Boat and Crew

The voyage begins. Just before the deluge, North Corfu

Doric Temple, Paestum

'Skyhook' fishnet, River Sele

A lonely cove just south of Capri

Night berth up the Sele River

The prize tunny catch

Low bridges were no problem: Sete

A lock at Beziers, Canal du Midi

The Calangues near Cassis

On the Canal du Midi

Goury, Cap de la Hague

In fact, I'm pretty good at it, managing before meals to bring my toes down to touch the ground, then springing them up again vertically, and it goes well about nine times out of ten. This morning was the tenth, and there I was rolling in the tinned tomatoes with the cooker upside down and a billy of good tea libating the beach.

I can see B.'s point of view, but there's no need to keep harping on.

'As if it isn't bad enough,' she splutters through the muslin turban she's wrapped round her head and face, 'to have sand in one's ears, one's nose, one's throat and the b— bed, without having it mixed with breakfast by the pound. What idiot other than my husband,' she goes on, 'would try to stand on his head while cooking breakfast? Just look at the butter.'

'I'm off to fill up the water canisters,' I retort, rubbing a very sore vertebra, and rattle off with the two jerrycans. Now the 'farm' which was the home of our beach host is about a hundred yards back in an apricot orchard. It is a quite delightful old place and the father of the family does not appear to be in residence. The mother, who presides, keeps house for her two stalwart sons, one of whom helped us pull *Lugworm* up the beach. He is a fine athletic young man, dark, well-proportioned, and susceptible to beauty. I know this because I happened to be watching his face when he first looked at B. yesterday. You know the sort of thing I mean – natural bonhomie tinged with the belligerence which operates between two male strangers can be seen to capsize and grow spongy round the edges when it comes face to face with glamour. Not that I'd call B. glamorous, but she has a certain something.

I like Alphonse, for such we have come to call him, having no idea of his real name, but suspect that he looks upon me as being something of a pity. Anyway, I found Alphonse sur-rounded by hens sweeping up what looked like the leftovers of battle, hundreds of purple squashed mulberries dropped overnight from a magnificent tree outside the farmhouse door – and here am I presenting myself with the two empty water cans.

'*Buongiorno, Signore,*' I address him. '*Per favour e... aqua fresco?*'

He surveys me for a moment looking a little glum, and disappears into the house. '*Un momento!*'

I sit under the mulberry tree with the hens. After a few minutes he reappears with a wheelbarrow and an empty five gallon drum. '*Vieni qua,*' he beckons. I follow him a little puzzled.

'Is there no water in the house? *Aqua ... non ... in casa?*' I query in my atrocious Italian. With a jerk of his head he indicates up the hills behind. '*Sulla salita,*' he says, and trundles on.

It is a long trundle, but interesting for all that. The gravel track winds through orange and lemon trees, olives and vines, then turns inland towards the hills; and I begin to feel more than a little embarrassed at having put our host to such trouble.

'*Scusi.*' I say, trying to convey my feeling. '*Non lo so non c'e aqua in casa ... pardone ... quanto chilometro in monte?*' I might be speaking Greek for all he understands, and probably was, so we just trundle on in silence until the track, which has now deteriorated to a narrow footpath bestrewn with boulders, ends at a small but fast flowing spring. A length of rigid plastic pipe lies nearby and this Alphonse places in the spring source, putting my jerrycans under the far end. There is enough fall to make the water flow. It is clever – but slow.

Meanwhile we sit and think, but not for long. From somewhere above us in the hills comes the distant wail of a siren. It increases in volume, finally arriving in a crescendo round a bend of the road, and there goes the top of a police car for a fleeting moment before it wails away with a ghastly Doppler effect on up the coast. This is shortly followed by a quite incredible sight: hordes of bottoms, jerking like puppets, flash into view, preceded by heads bent low. A holocaust of cyclists pedalling as though Hell were in pursuit, legions of them, interspersed with police motorcycles, the occasional siren blaring, radio phones crackling; endlessly they stream round the hillside above, and I look at my host questioningly.

'*Vicino la Sicilia Internationale race di bicycletta,*' he says, and seeing my incomprehension tries it in English. 'Beechicletta Internationalie', and then, continues, 'Chuko Vin Sore ... you hear?'

I ponder that one. Chuko vin sore? Chukovin, Sore? Chu kovin sore? Chuko vinsore ... ?

Blankly I look at him. He tries again, putting tremendous emphasis into the words ... 'CHUKO VIN SORE ... YOU!'

Suddenly it clicks. DUKE OF WINDSOR! It must be. But what on earth has that got to do with a round Sicily Bicycle Rally? Can it be – and I look up the hills to where the last broad backside is palpitating away in the distance – can it possibly be that the old boy is heading the Rally? No ... it's just ridiculous. Perhaps sponsoring it; well, it's possible I suppose; good old Royalty, they really are getting democratic; but somehow it seems doubtful. Alphonse is standing now, looking frustrated. Once more he tries.

'YOU ... CHUKO VINSOR ... E MORTO OGGI,' He stamps the ground with exasperation. 'MISSUS SIMPSONE AT QUEEN. CHUKO VINSOR E MORTO.'

Morto! There is a bell clanging far away down in the village. Can it really be that cracked, or is it just the effect of distance?

Morto! Is this Sicilian youngster trying to tell me that the Duke of Windsor is dead and Mrs Simpson is at the Palace?

Soon it is quite clear that this is precisely what he is so desperately trying to make me understand. But why, I am wondering with half my mind, why should he bother? I look away up the hills. Below me the cracked bell is still ringing – why, I wonder? Behind us the cicadas are making the midday heat crackle with their strident chirruping, and the Duke of Windsor is dead.

Goodness, I wish that bell would stop. What memories are floating slowly up this far-off hillside with that distant sad cracked note. So the young King Edward the Eighth is no more, and the woman he loved is finally accepted at the Palace.

Bizarre, kaleidoscopic world. Here on this hot Sicilian hillside, strangely enough I just want to sit down and cry.

*   *   *

If you happened to be working your way north before a brisk westerly close under the lee of that remarkable promontory which ends in Cape Milazzo on the north Sicilian shore, as we were that morning of the last day in May, you would see on the horizon a truly impressive sight. The volcanic cone of Stromboli, balanced like an inverted pudding basin, seems to tower into the heavens, over thirty miles away. Dark pewter against the incredible blue of the sky, it wears round its peak, like a monk's tonsure, a white fringe of cloud. The nearer islands of Vulcano, Lipari, Salina and Panarea are hidden behind the end of the promontory, and Stromboli alone rears like a forbidding sentinel ahead. There is something strangely brooding about the hunch of its shoulders and the regular incline of its three thousand foot high slopes, but the most impressive thing about this natural vent is the small plume of smoke and steam which, regular as clockwork, every half hour or so, fingers its way vertically above the cone, to disperse quickly in the clear sky.

It is as though one were watching a vast sleeping monster which, now and then, exhales a long and sulphurous breath. The mind boggles at the possibility of a cough, sneeze, or more violent awakening and the eye can become hypnotised by the sight, counting minutes till the next horribly portentous puff. Totally absorbed in this phenomenon as I was, you might just excuse me (B. never will) for ramming the rock which brought the noble *Lugworm* crashing to a standstill – anchored firmly by the bottom of her rudderblade.

In fact, so firmly was she pinioned that her after parts were lifted six inches or so above her normal water-level. We leapt forward, in an effort to bear down on her bow, thus allowing the stern to float free, but to no avail. I looked cautiously over the side. Sure enough, there was the weedy top of a large rock, towering up from the depths, and here was *Lugworm* staked like a banner to its crest. You may wonder why I did not simply lift the rudder from its trunking, but alas, this was impossible for the violence of impact had bent the sprung steel rudderpost beyond removal. There was nothing for it: I gingerly lowered myself on to the weedy pinnacle and with B. perched at the bow, I forcibly shoved her ample quarters inch by inch until she finally slid off the pinnacle and floated free.

A dive under the surface revealed the worst – the post was badly bent. It presented problems, for while it was still possible to move the helm and thus steer the boat, she could no longer be beached, since before doing so the rudder has to be unshipped. If possible, the post would have to be straightened while the rudder was still in position, and with womanly logic B. suggested that, since we had bent it the one way by impact in a forward direction, surely the obvious thing was to bend it the opposite way by impact in a reverse direction.

101

I thought about that. There seemed no harm in trying and, after all, the post might not need to be straightened completely in order to be withdrawn. If we could just bash it somewhere near true we might be able to unship it, beach, and finish the job properly. We dropped all sail, relocated the rock, and lowered the outboard. In principle the problem was easy – all we had to do was to hold the helm roughly amidships and ram the rock with the back of the rudderblade stern-first. But things are never as simple as they appear. To begin with, in order to get sternway on we had to use the outboard motor, and maintain a high degree of steerage in order to strike the rock correctly. That meant the outboard had to be stopped and locked into the up position just before impact, otherwise there was every chance of wrecking the engine.

Meanwhile, on the shore close by, people were beginning to take an interest. The obvious fact that a boat has struck a rock is enough to attract anyone's attention, but the chance of seeing a circus act such as we were putting on was drawing an interested crowd.

'This way,' a voice cried, beckoning us into the beach. Others took up the cry, and free advice was offered as to the best channel in through the off-lying rocks. Of course they could not know this was the one thing we dare not attempt until the rudder had been unshipped. Again and again we reversed on to that blessed rock, while the onlookers, gathering verbal momentum became enraged at the sight of what must have seemed deliberate boaticide.

It was no use. Poor *Lugworm* staggered repeatedly under the impacts, but that steel rod laughed at our efforts and remained just as bent. There was only one thing for it, the tiller head had to be taken off and the rudder dropped down free of the keel from underneath and obviously, this had to be done in fairly shallow water, or there was every chance of losing the blade and post complete. We anchored in a depth of six feet and I dived under her stern, making a light line fast to the blade with a barrel-hitch. Then, by easing back the tiller head clamp bolt the blade was lowered until the top end of its post came free of the keel. After that, we were able to nose our way into the boisterous group and explain the complexities of our problem.

But how were we to straighten that post? Sicilians and Italians as a people tend to be warm, open-hearted and helpful, but they are also highly volatile and hold very firm opinions. If these opinions happen to be at variance with one another it is quite possible for the fact to spark off physical violence; even about helping to straighten a stupid foreigner's bent rudder post.

I started with the best will in the world to clout the bent post with a heavy rock, but such was the quality of that steel that the rock simply sprung out of my hand on impact, singing its own glad song as it went.

This intrigued the crowd, who quickly grew impatient at this obvious ineptitude and finally a powerful man strode forward, tapped me on the shoulder and took the rudder out of my hands with an air of a father quietly taking charge from an incompetent child. He took it, followed by the crowd, down the beach and carefully selected a narrow crack between two massive boulders. Jamming the post firmly into this crack, he grasped the blade between both arms, braced his feet against the base of one rock and gently started to apply force. His muscles bulged, the veins stood out on his neck and a suffused red glow spread over his determined face. At the moment of full effort, the blade, under tremendous stress, sprang round and flung our friend full length in the shingle; the rudder remained bent and juddering gently in the crack.

— IF A SICILIAN COULDN'T...!

Undaunted our friend picked himself up, took a deep breath and advanced again to the task, encouraged and goaded by the advice and criticisms of the crowd. The business was now completely out of our hands – the straightening of the rudder-post was a matter of personal if not national prestige, and if a Sicilian couldn't bend back a bit of paltry English steel, what was he good for, eh?

Again the post was firmly jammed between the rocks, and this time a friend of the friend was positioned to preclude that blade swinging round under stress. Again muscles bulged. An awed silence fell on the crowd, as gradually one rock separated from the other, the crack widened and the post, still just as bent, claimed a second victory. But now the entire crowd was clearly on its mettle. Somebody appeared brandishing a car jack. Loud discussion took place, most of it quite incomprehensible to us, and the offending rudder was carted across

104

the road to a nearby garden where a high stone wall abutted the end of a house. At the end of this wall was a slot – a sort of vertical drain hole – left between the solid boulders of the footings. It was ingenious, the whole idea. The blade was hammered, not without trouble, deep into this slot, leaving the offending post sticking from the wall. Thus jammed, and firmly held, the blade could not twist round, and the jack was then positioned under the post. The garden was crammed full of people. B. and I were awed watchers of this clever ruse. The house owner smiled at us; the jack owner's lips were thin and determined, the friend and the friend of the friend just glowered.

Slowly the jack was tensioned; the post was seen to start bending like a clock spring, in a graceful curve; a hush fell on the watchers. Little by little that inch and an eighth diameter steel post bent up and then, unbelievably the slot elongated, its lintel stone rising up to carry the entire wall with it. Seconds later we were looking at a gaping hole, and all Hell was let loose. Everybody was shouting at everybody else.

The friend and the friend of the friend were rolling about with laughter until the houseowner actually hit one of them. I extricated the still triumphant rudder and together we withdrew, making every kind of apologetic noise to anyone who was prepared to listen; but nobody seemed interested in us any longer. Why should they be – wasn't there a full scale war getting into gear back there in the garden?

We re-embarked, and motored gingerly out through the rocks, the still bent rudder grinning at us from the bottom boards, and it took me two solid hours in a secret place with a borrowed eight pound sledgehammer to persuade that post back far enough for it to once again be inserted in the normal manner. Aha! I would give a lot to know exactly where that rudder and tiller is right now. But that is another story which will be told in good time.

*   *   *

Vulcano, which rose from the sea in 183 B.C., is famous for its therapeutic mud. It may be famous for other things as well, but so far as I'm concerned the mud's enough—it's quite splendid. One earthy ambition of a friend of mine is to watch well proportioned women wrestling in mud, and I quite agree with him; there's something wonderfully erotic about the whole idea. It may be why I'm sitting up to my neck in this boghole.

We sailed the fifteen miles to the island yesterday evening after that fiasco with the rudder, and really life has been hilarious since we anchored here in the Baia di Levante. To begin with, the sea is constantly belching; it leaves no shadow of doubt that we're fossicking about on sufferance here, and it makes you appreciate the present. Sulphurous gases pop up from the bottom and *Lugworm* has spent the night anchored in the bay with her belly being tickled. It sounded pleasant enough inside, like floating in a glass of champagne, but the smell takes a bit of getting used to. You either like it or you don't; I'm not sure myself.

These mudholes are like small lakes, scooped out of the low-lying shore not far from the sea, and they look as though they have been messed about a bit by man, but don't think the mud is black – far from it. White would be nearer the mark. Battleship grey is about the right colour, and the occupants are totally disenchanting. One sits and hopes, but so far the nearest thing to a sex symbol is two obese German Fraus down at the far end who, with appalling concentration, are laving themselves with hands full of the stuff.

106

Apart from a dreadfully ill-looking Italian paddling about in another hole, that's it. And me. But I'm just a head sticking out. The heat is terrific, you have to prod about carefully to select a tolerable spot and lie full length to get completely covered because it's quite shallow, but if you're going to get in you might as well get right in not friggle about. I've been gently simmering here for half an hour and there are still no well-proportioned women, much less any chance of a wrestling match so I might as well go and give B. a shock. She's still turned-in.

I drag myself out, all slimy grey and shining, and flap along the beach, slap sluppy slop it's DELIGHTFUL! If I stick my elbows out, it doesn't make so much noise. 'B.,' I yell from the beach. 'Quick, look at this.'

I know what a shock it was; a near black head sticking out from a light grey mudpack. I have the photo beside me as I type. You want to see it? Well you can't – it's positively revolting.

B. is not impressed. But the mud is drying. Even as I stand in the sun it's beginning to congeal.

'I'm going to run round the island to see what happens,' I call to her, and set off. It's fantastic; have you ever run fast completely encased in a thick layer of drying mud? No, I bet you haven't. I blunder into a family emerging from a chalet and a small child screams and sits down suddenly. The mother rushes over protectively and the whole group stands gaping as I disappear. Better not to stop now, they might think I'm mad. On I go, but it's hardening quickly – almost like glue. When my thighs hit each other they stick together and it's most uncomfortable – better to run with my legs apart.

Have you ever tried running with your elbows out and yours legs apart? It's hilarious. Dammit there's another group right across the path; a portly gentleman (Lord, he could be Eng-

107

lish) grabs a beach brolly and freezes at the head of the column, like Napoleon. What does he think I'm going to do: attack him? It's difficult enough running like this, never mind getting belligerent. Why do they all stare so – you'd think I was stark naked. The mud is cracking and dropping off in cakes. It's getting a bit uncomfortable so I stand on my head just for fun, and I bet you've never done that, either, caked in mud. Oh, it's quite a morning one way and another.

I run right round Vulcanello at the north of the island to have another look at Stromboli. Then take a swim in the hot bubbling water, wipe the lot off and join B. for breakfast.

Halfway through coffee she pokes her head out of the tent. 'Why are all those people standing on the beach looking at us?' she enquires.

It's true; there are dozens of them, standing in groups gaping at us.

'Maybe they've never seen a boat like *Lugworm* before.' I comfort her, and carry on with the marmalade.

Yes, it's been a surprisingly different morning, one way and another. Better than the eight-fifteen.

*   *   *

It's no distance at all from Vulcano to the Island of Lipari – half a mile across a twenty fathom strait and you're there. This is the island which in ancient times was known as Meligunis and is the largest of the archipelago, famous of old as a trading centre for obsidian, the dark vitreous lava that looks like broken glass bottles. Today its most remarkable sight is the quarries in the pumice hills, above Canneto on the eastern shore: for all the world like our Cornish china clay mines. The sea round these isles is thick with floating pumice, you can scoop up knobbles of it everywhere.

The sixteenth-century Spanish fortress above the small port is magnificent. If you want to float back in time, just drift around the narrow streets of the town behind the castle; no hideous din of internal combustion engines and at night, when the litter from the tourists seems less obvious, it's quite enchanting. After you have lost yourself in the history of the place you may wander out and lose yourself in the deep valleys that run up the steep hills behind. On the western shore the small road runs high on the cliff tops and one can look from Quattrocchi (four eyes and well-named for you really need them), down at a superb coastline with magnificent off-lying rocks. It's great fun to wander about looking at the coast then to be able to say, 'Come on, let's go and sail round there!' But yesterday *Lugworm* got her anchor jammed under some massive boulders thirty feet down – we could see it for two hours while we tried every conceivable way of recovering it other than hiring an aqua lung. After that it just came free, but it was a good opportunity to explore the depths with our snorkel gear and flippers. Phew … but it's hot on this hillside and the sulphurous smell everywhere seems to make it even more humid, one begins to feel over-ripe if you know what I mean, like a soft tomato. It would be good to have this scenery and sunshine with an occasional bracing Cornish wind, but one can't have everything and I mustn't grumble, we're doing pretty well.

I think the most noticeable thing about these islands is the peace. We have forgotten what life must have been like before machinery was invented. No noise, and none of that hysterical rushing about that internal combustion engines engender. A good place to escape and be happy in, these Aeolian Isles. It's a strange thing, happiness, people say you can be happy anywhere – I can't. To be happy I've always thought I had to be surrounded by beauty and tranquillity, but is this really true?

When you look at these islands they are not very beauti-ful. Great lumps of volcanic ash probing up from the sea have little grace. Grandeur, yes. Tranquillity? Perhaps, but it is a brooding tranquillity – unimaginable power at rest. What makes them so enchanting is the colours. You have to experience this to know what I'm talking about. The sky in the evening is inde-scribable. It almost lifts you out of reality into a dream world of fantasy: you see the evening light on the western flanks of the hills, infusing a luminous glow into the subtle greens of the fig, cypress, olive and cactus, and behind it all is the dark reds and violets of the lava and black volcanic ash. The powdered ash of the beaches is that pure matt of lamp-black, it takes a bit of getting used to. Of course there is novelty value for northern Europeans like us, the warmth alone tends to wrap all other ex-periences with a blanket of content. But one wonders how long the indolence and non-action, the sheer hedonistic pleasure of sunbathing and swimming here, divorced from all the roots of one's own culture, the stimulation of the colder climate, the very scents of England, could withstand a dreadful ennui; a vacuum of non-creativity.

Pondering on happiness, I remember a thought from some-where way back in my schooldays, which for me seemed and still seems to capture something of its meaning. I am an Eng-lishman, wondering in a far off place whether I could really remain happy anywhere else than at home. It runs:

Happiness … ?
Happiness lies in the crook of a willow
Down near the pool where the cows stand at dusk
Deep in the heart of a wood fire at night.
Happiness lies wherever the green of a hill meets the sky
Where leaves that are new can tremble and shiver

And wind lifts the song of a lark on high.
It lies in the warm grass whose breath has been freed
By the soft swinging low singing glide of a scythe
and comes with the river
the reedy rush river
the watercress river
… and sun in my eyes.

Well … is that England? Or is it perhaps the ghost of England? How often today does one catch the scent of meadow grass drying in the sun, freed by the 'soft swinging low singing glide of a scythe' on the banks of 'the reedy rush river, the watercress river?' It is still there in odd corners of course, but mostly it has been overtaken by the characterless face of 'progress', buried beneath the concrete and tarmacadam of the motorway systems, with their foetid breath of carbon monoxide. Can one still, I wonder, ever catch a fleeting shadow of it in our darkened homes with the stark flicker of the 'box' – watching the hysterical animal violence of the crowds at soccer matches? – listening to the eternal reports of union wrangling with management, political squabbles, violence?

One wonders sometimes what is the value of our 'gains' compared with the price we are paying in terms of loss. One wonders sometimes if England really exists any longer, if soon there really will be any roots left to go back to.

But these are sombre thoughts for a sunny hillside on Lipari, altogether too close to reality for pleasantness, so come on, let's go down and get some sail on *Lugworm*; it's a fair soft silent south wind and we can ghost up to Panarea before nightfall.

*   *   *

Panarea is delightful, for my money the best of the islands we had yet seen; no cars, just a few three-wheel drays for delivering stores from the boats that ply out to meet the inter-island steamers. What development has taken place is in good taste, nothing even remotely trippery. Long may it stay so. There is no real harbour, just a mole on the north-east shore giving protection to a beach of large boulders, and there is a small sandy beach to the south-east. The western shore has dramatic steep cliffs and the rest of the island is really a natural garden with rhododendrons, figs, eucalyptus trees and a riot of geraniums. There is a form of hollyhock too, and cactus. It is interesting to see that all the fishing boats, some of them a lot larger than *Lugworm*, are regularly pulled out up the stony beaches, sliding over wooden baulks like railway sleepers.

We had a delicious evening meal ashore in a quiet and homely restaurant overlooking *Lugworm*; fish soup and *spaghetti con pommodoro* in company with the twelve apostles hanging on the wall – a picture of the Last Supper. Before turning in we shifted *Lugworm* to the other end of the bay, and though the weather generally remained calm, the night was made remarkable by the most peculiar violent gusts of wind coming off the island. It made sleeping afloat with the tent rigged most intriguing. When the wind hit her, *Lugworm* ranged about, chuckling to herself, which B. found most disturbing, imagining that we were adrift and disappearing out to sea. 'That would be fun,' I comforted her, but she didn't seem at ease.

The early forecast next morning gave the sea as *'poco mosso'* (slight) and sky as *'sereno o poco nuvoloso'* (clear or slight cloud) with winds light from the north. In fact, at 0930 a splendid north westerly came fanning along. We reached, under genoa, main and mizzen, out past the offlying islet of Basiluzzo and there was Stromboli, much larger now, eight miles to the north east. 'We seem to have been looking at it for a long time,' B. said to me after breakfast, 'Are we actually going to land on it today?'

It was a spanking good sail. I remember we reached across with genoa set, arriving about midday close to a tiny concrete slipway hidden in the rocks just west of Punta Monaco on the south shore. A small dinghy lay on the slip but swell and sea was churning the narrow approach into a foam bath. We continued running goosewinged up the eastern shore, losing the wind progressively as we edged into the lee of the island. Soon we were ghosting lazily within feet of the black cinder beaches, and it was while silently studying the high shoulders of the volcano that we first heard the awe-inspiring far-off rumble, like a reverberation of distant thunder. It echoed and re-echoed, dropping gently down from the heights like a suppressed growl from earth herself. We looked at each other and remained silent, awed by the sheer power of it.

By early evening we were becalmed off the north-east shore just to the south of the village. There was no harbour, nor even a mole – just the incredibly black beach sloping to the water's edge, then plunging on down for more than a thousand fathoms; a terrible place to be caught in bad weather. But the barometer was steady and all seemed fair and set calm so we decided to remain afloat and dropped our bow anchor a few feet from the beach, taking the stern anchor well onshore. One or two dirty white box-like houses were straggled about a hundred yards back, and beyond these we could see a few more scattered dwellings rising up the fields of vines, and the deeper green of a lemon grove, while higher up we could see the dried coarse grasses and broom, gently merging into the brown and reddish solidified lava which towered on up into the sky itself. No sound broke the oppressive silence other than the long gentle surge of the sea along the beach, and then, again, came that distant hollow and all-pervading rumble.

'I don't like this place,' B. whispered, looking up there to where the faint echoes of the sound still lingered. 'It makes me feel too vulnerable, too small to even matter; it's frightening.'

'True,' I agreed.' But in a way it's salutory for we microbes who think ourselves Lords of the Earth and the Universe.' I was remembering Santorini, that relic of a volcanic cataclysm in the south Aegean where we had recently spent a month living in a pumice cave and where 3,500 years before, eighty square kilometres of mountain top had blown sky high leaving the sea to flood the vast crater, wiping out the Minoan civilization in Crete and bringing death and destruction along the seaboard of the entire Aegean with the resultant mountainous waves. In our position, at the foot of this other monster, it didn't bear dwelling on.

'Still,' I said out loud, 'if an entire village can live their lives here, I'm prepared to accept the risk of one or two days. Come on, let's have a brew of tea and then find out what's going on up there?' Within half an hour we were ashore enquiring as to the best ascent.

The village was a pleasant surprise, there was a tranquil charm about the narrow lanes which led between the small houses, each with its little garden bursting with red geraniums. As usual there were no cars. We passed a sleepy white church and the occasional donkey dozing in the late afternoon heat, and one or two small shops which seemed to differ little from the private houses, save for the wares displayed in the windows. An elderly man, hacking patiently with a broad bladed adze at a small field of dry black soil, stopped his work and, with quiet courtesy indicated the best way to the summit, pointing towards the far end of the village. We wandered on following the lane until it escaped from the confines of the houses and stretched itself, a wide stone pathway now, zig-zagging up the gentle lower slopes, and giving the impression that one was wandering through hanging gardens, so thick and rich with yellow flowers was the broom.

After about half an hour of steady climbing, the path, which was beautifully made of cut stone blocks, became narrower and more unkempt. About five hundred feet up we sat and looked back. Far away, over the distant village we could still see *Lugworm*, a mere dot on the fringe of black shore snugged close under the foot of this vast cinder heap – a ridiculous speck in an eternity of blue sea and sky which stretched out to a horizon made vastly more distant by our height.

But there remained more than two thousand five hundred feet to be climbed, and having no fancy to be caught on the slopes in darkness we hastened on at greater pace while the path became more haphazard, carried away in places by small landslides. It wound through a bamboo grove, broke clear and snaked across a steep shoulder of low scrub, finally shaking off all semblance of respectability as a man-made track to become a lithe impatient beaten cinder path, ever steeper as it attacked the slopes in a more direct line to the top.

Another hour of this, and B. decided she had had enough. We had spent it clambering across the loose metallic sounding clinker, clinging to the illusive path then losing it again. For every step forward we slid half a step back. Both of us were hot and growing tired, but the view lifted us high above such mundanities. We had reached a point where a ridge dropped vertically about fifty feet. Below this the slope inclined away at a steady sixty degree angle of black clinker scree sheer for two thousand feet before plunging under the blue-green sea. It was an awesome sight, appalling for anyone who suffers from vertigo, and it was here that B. sat down and stated that her legs had gone to jelly and she intended climbing no farther. 'You go on,' she said, I'll regain my breath and then start slowly back down and you can overtake me when you've seen the crater.'

At that moment the volcano 'blew' again. But this time we heard it building up, now frighteningly close, like the approach of a mighty wind, then I swear the ground itself shook and there came that spine chilling roar which left us looking feebly at the white plume of smoke rising so tantalizingly near up there.

'That's it,' she said. I'm off; this is no place for a girl with imagination – goodbye, and please be back before dark. I shall worry.'

With that she started scrambling down and I watched until her tiny figure disappeared over a bluff, far below, and then I again looked upwards. The clinker slopes, broken here and there by outcrops of contorted purple lava towered into the sky. There was another thousand feet still to go and I had no idea whether it was possible to get to the crater edge or not. For that matter I didn't know whether I was on the right path or whether this apology for a track finally disappeared up there in a mountainside of scree. What happened after that? Would the clinker get too hot for my bare feet? When the crater 'blew', did it blow out a bit more lava and ash as well – and where was I going to be if it did? If I was not to be scorched alive and buried it would have to be well outside its range, and how far was that? In nothing but a swimsuit, it was all a bit disconcerting and quite exciting really. Odd what a difference being alone makes to one's courage. I was fighting the desire to scoot down there after B. and call it a day, but couldn't think of any reason for doing so other than being a coward, so I started climbing again to stop the thinking.

116

If it gets too hot, I thought, I'll have a good excuse to go back. Now do I, or don't I hope it gets too hot? My mind bumbled on to itself as I scrabbled over the loose resonant stuff. A thousand vertical feet is an awful lot of clinker. Suppose my weight starts an avalanche – just a few billion tons of it sliding down. I suppose they'll cast an idle glance up from the village and carry on milking the goat and that'll be that, with me just an undetectable redder splodge on the hillside of congealed magma. Would it matter?

At last the infernal slope began to level off. I stopped scrabbling about like a monkey on all fours and stood erect and there ahead of me was another entire mountain. Have you ever had that experience? When you're certain you have finally reached the peak and there you stand again looking up from a new lot of foothills! Dammit, I thought, unless that Admiralty Chart is lying, there cannot be more than another seven hundred and fifty feet left before I'm flying.

But gently, as I rested there to regain energy and breath, there stole across the scene a remarkable change. The vanguard of that monk's tonsure came creeping silently round the slope alongside to envelop it and me. The effect was dramatic. Gone was the oven hot bright limitless world, the blazing distant blues and nearby cinder reds and browns; instead I was in a dreadfully cold closed twilight of greys and blacks, with the damp swirling mist goosepimpling my hide, and as I shivered there a strange lurid freak of the thin light began to take effect all round. It was as though the black slopes of the volcano were glowing with a green luminescence. It may have been the damp glistening on the sulphurous clinker, or it could have been something to do with over-compensation within my eyes adjusting to the sudden change of light, colour and intensity, but the whole swirling cold and hollow world up there in the heights took on this lurid luminous green shimmer as though the ash were carpeted with glistening moss. But this was not just the effect of the light and cloud; the dark slopes were actually smoking, or it may have been steam rising where the mist touched the hot ashes, but the green glow was reflected from acres and acres of rising tongues of mist, like green flames, and over all there hung a suffocating oppressive smell of sulphur.

I wanted to drop down, quickly, and get out of that cloud level, back to the bright real world below. Visibility was down to a few hundred yards in this subterranean world of the sky, and then a thought came to me; maybe I was an idiot, but wouldn't it be as easy to break up above that cloud level, as it would be to drop below it? I knew, having seen the volcano from afar, that there was almost always a small peak standing proud of the clouds.

Shivering with the cold, I picked my way steadily upwards. The world seemed to be getting darker, and there was a wind now, drifting the cloud perceptibly past. To my right there seemed to be an overall gloom and through a sudden slight rift in the mist I saw that I was in a valley, a narrow black valley with a thin line of path along the bottom. I started to run, and the path began to incline upwards away from the valley base, sloping round the shoulder of the hill. It was dank and cold and the smell was overpowering.

Suddenly, as though dark curtains were being drawn aside, my closed world grew bright again, its boundaries rolling back and away. I was still running hard up the path, round the shoulder of a small hillock of ash when I broke free from that fast retreating cloud.

But how can I describe the scene? I was alone in the sky on a tiny black smoking island surrounded by a sea of snow white cloud. Down below me on all sides, obscuring the horizon of the real sea, was a swirling ocean of fast moving white billows, and there was nothing else in the whole world save this small island which appeared to be flowing along through its billowing sea, floating in a universe of intensely dark blue sky. I stood on the peak of a small hummock and spread my arms to the wonderful warmth of that sun. Truly, I felt I could have flown at that moment, alone up there above the world on this magic carpet in the sky; indeed, I seemed to be flying as I ran on, following the thin winding track. It balanced along a knife ridge, the slopes of which plunged down on both sides to disappear beneath that misty sea; I knew how many thousand feet it went down, down, invisibly beneath the cloud, but that world down there no longer existed for me. I ran, light as air, through a rainbow of steam, up a rise and down a long gradual incline, breasted the brow of another rise – and came to a halt, aghast.

Fifty yards ahead, standing on the very edge of the great crater, were two women dressed in heavy tweeds, thick stockings and tough brogues. One carried an open umbrella and the other had a guide book under one arm and a camera round her neck.

'You looked exactly like Eros,' the woman said, in a horsey English voice. 'Running down that hill, with practically nothing on. How ever can you do it in bare feet, I don't know?' and she looked me up and down as one might view a cod on a fishslab. Obviously, I was quite beyond her comprehension. But she was talking still.

'You're only just in time if you've come to see the puff. It's due in precisely one minute – that's why we've got the umbrella.' Her friend smiled weakly, adjusted her spectacles and examined the camera.

'We must leave immediately it's over, Agatha,' she burbled on. 'We simply must not miss the evening boat. And I must

119

say I'll not be sorry, they really ought to put a fence round this hole!'

I stood there, and I swear I could actually hear the fabric of my world of light in the sky crumbling and collapsing around me. Suddenly, there came a quite unreasonable anger welling up. Damn and blast and damn you, I shouted silently in my mind, smiling sweetly at her. Is NOWHERE on earth free of bloody tourists, here, of all places! – and I turned away, lest my eyes should give me away.

Hell's bowels, but I was angry.

From the ruins of another world, I started to laugh. 'There's a good flat place for a car park back there,' I commented. 'They might allow, perhaps, a slight discount for coaches?' I added mildly, to be met with an uncomprehending stare.

Suddenly, I didn't want at all to stand there while mother Earth did her little show for the clicking cameras of the tourists. Somehow it all seemed beneath her dignity. I hoped she would belch a gurgle of molten bowel and vaporise the screaming tweed, socks, brogues, me and all.

'I'm off!' I roared and they both jumped as I pelted back up that path, round the shoulder and back down the gloomy valley. I was halfway through the cloud layer when the earth herself began to roar too. I heard it grumbling up from somewhere deep in her belly underfoot, rumbling closer and closer with a noise like a small hurricane, and then with a booming akin to a thousand express trains neck and neck in a tunnel she spewed again. A cloud of warm ash began to rain down, and I was covered in ochre grit. But oh, I was so angry – angry with myself, the world, and everybody in it. Fool, Duxbury, I fumed within, don't you know that you're living in the twentieth century, not some greater ideal Homeric world of another age. Come down to earth you idiot; they've as much right to be up there as you have.

120

But I wish they hadn't been. I was so angry I ran all the way back down, one and a half hours aided by gravity, and was still fuming when I overtook B. just outside the village.

'You've been very quick,' she said, startled as I came padding along. 'Did you see the blow?'

I sat down on the path and told her exactly how it had all happened, how it had all been so wonderful, and how it had all suddenly collapsed in a packet of English Tweed.

'Oh B.,' I groaned, still fuming. 'I really got very very near to Heaven up there; for a moment it was unbelievably wonderful.'

I sat and regained my breath there on the path, until a strange sound made me look aside. B. was lying full-length in the grass, holding her sides and rolling about, with laughter.

I suppose it's why I love her so.

*   *   *

Our earth has long since turned this face from the sun, carrying us here on Stromboli far into the lee of night. Only the glow of our candle under the cotton awning traps a pale memory of day, and the sea, whispering softly on the ash beach, begins to lull us towards sleep.

But we are roused by the crunch of footsteps. Two figures have left the village and now, at the top of the rise they have lit a fisherman's pressure lamp which hangs over the stern of a boat hauled high. They carry wide rakes, and when the lamp is burning well, move down to the water's edge nearby and commence raking the black beach flat, forming a level highway up to another boat which rests on wooden sleepers well above sea level. Two or three more figures emerge from the village, and then a drift of ten or so in a group, some of them carrying rucksacks, some with rolled bedding across their backs. Teenagers mostly, young men and women, they gather at the top of the beach round the boat with the lamp. Their figures cast long moving shadows which drift across the distant dim faces of the houses, erasing them to join the blackness of night for a fleeting moment. There are more groups forming behind the lamp, and we see a rope being led from the boat on sleepers down the beach.

Amid the hum of conversation a voice rises. The murmur dies for a moment, then rises again as a surge of people move down the beach to grasp the rope. A figure – it is a girl – leaps on to the boat with the lamp and puts a tin whistle to her lips; the thin reedy notes come floating across, and a voice picks up the tune, followed by more and more as the crowd take up the ditty. Soon everybody on the beach is singing lustily, and with the swing of the tune they put their weight on the rope. Others crowd round the boat, which begins to slide towards the sea.

Two black shadows vie with one another to collect the sleepers from astern and thrust them again beneath the bow of the moving boat, forming a ramp down which she can slide to the water, and the singing rises in tempo as the crowd begins to catch the rhythm.

But above it all now comes another sound; it is a deep regular throb, like a quick pulse from somewhere out there in the black sea, and as we look across the water two bright eyes, one red and one green, can be seen making towards us. It is the ferry steamer from Milazzo approaching.

The haulers on the rope have now reached the waterline, and fold back to join the willing hands ranged round the boat. With a last cheer she is pushed forward, the crowd running alongside, until she plunges into the sea, while a dozen or so islanders grasp another line trailing from her stern and check the way, then pull her gently back to the beach. A plank is rigged and the still singing crowd begin to embark. The throb of the ship's propeller ceases suddenly and as the ship swings slowly round, the deck lights expand into a long bright necklace a quarter of a mile off, throwing their own faint light on the tableau on shore.

Now the boat is full, and amid shouts of farewell is shoved off from the beach, the long oars gripping the water as four lusty islanders pull towards the ship. Twice the boat returns, and each time she departs the figures on the beach thin out until, finally, only six islanders stand there waiting her final return in silence, their cigarettes glowing in the night. As the boat casts off for the last time from the ship, the vessel's engines throb once more into life, her lights swing away, and gradually disappear into the darkness.

I wade ashore and join the waiting islanders. A block has been overhauled to the water's edge, its tackle secured to a massive stake up the beach. And as the boat crunches into the ash this is hooked to her stem. Two each side, we keep the boat level on her broad keel as she is hauled slowly back up the beach. I drag the sleepers from the stern and thrust them under the moving bow. When she is far enough up, the tackle is unhooked and two stout chocks placed beneath her bilge. The pressure lamp is dowsed.

'*Grazie, Signore ... buonanotte,*' one of the islanders murmurs to me, and they drift back into the sleeping village. The ship is just a pale dot of light on the horizon.

Our candle glow leads me back to *Lugworm*, and the sigh of the sea on the ash beach lulls us both off to sleep.

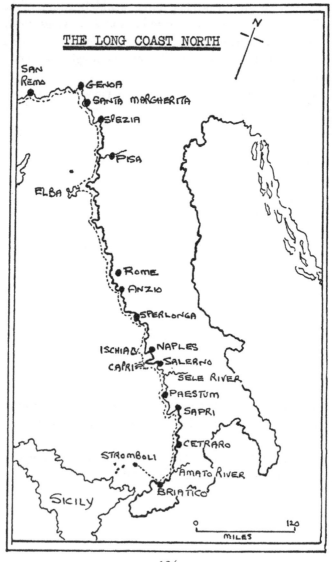

THE LONG COAST NORTH

SAN REMO
GENOA
SANTA MARGHERITA
SPEZIA
PISA
ELBA
Rome
ANZIO
SPERLONGA
ISCHIA
NAPLES
CAPRI
SALERNO
SELE RIVER
PAESTUM
SAPRI
CETRARO
STROMBOLI
AMATO RIVER
BRIATICO
SICILY

0   120
MILES

124

CHAPTER IV

The Long Coast North

WAS IT GEORGE BERNARD SHAW or Caesar who said that the art of life lies in gathering memories? I do not know, but I do know that memories, like good wine, last longer and remain clearer when stored in the right container – and what pure magic can lie enshrined in a chart! Sitting here writing late in the February night, with a log fire crackling and the good old English sleet slurrying on the window panes, I look at this battered faded sheet. Creased, scribbled on, stained with coffee and with the clear imprint of five small toes spread across the title, I trace the familiar names, each rich with memories, of that Calabrian coastline; feel again the blazing heat of the sun, shade my eyes from the blinding light on untold beaches, and see the faint silhouettes of the distant islands. I turn the page of our log, and begin to read.

It is forty-three miles from Stromboli to Vibo Valentia on the Italian mainland. The first thirty-odd are across open sea and then you connect with that carbuncle on the Italian toe which comes to a head at Cape Vaticano. It's far enough in a dinghy – one is well advised to pick the weather carefully and Ye Gods, we couldn't have bettered this day if we had rigged the Heavenly computer.

Stromboli still looms twelve miles astern, crowned with that ridiculous wisp of mist, but now the blue haze of distance has robbed the volcano of its power. If it erupts at this moment we shall merely be entertained by a firework display and, being totally human, it no longer seems to matter much.

But the sea – how I wish you could be here! From horizon to horizon is a tranquil plate of blue with no trace of wind to so much as ripple the surface: no single puff of cloud is mirrored there from the high blue bowl of sky, and the monotonous throb of our outboard thrusts *Lugworm* gently on, making the tiny whirlpools swirl from under her counter where deeps of ten hundred fathoms paint a darker mauve-blue void. The whirlpools spin, flatten and grow irregular down either side of the wake, finally dissolving in limpid ennui as they too give up the struggle and pass into oblivion. Indeed, we are finding it hard to fight off sleep in this baking blue world of sun and sea and sky.

I count the crystal beads of water strung like diamonds on our fishing line astern and for the hundredth time haul it in hopefully. The spinner winks idly at me. 'Do you really think any damned fish will make the effort to give chase on a day like this?' it seems to say, and I drop it back, half envious of its silver path through the cool silent depths. We stretch out in our nothings, settling down to a soporific stupor as the sun mounts higher, adding yet another shade of tan to our already mahogany skins.

All things considered, we are keeping remarkably healthy and fit on this venture. It's surprising really because the fresh water is becoming a bit of a problem. Plastic cans are perhaps not the best containers for storing drinking water in a hot climate, but at least they have one big advantage: if they're thin and white like ours they do allow one to detect the colour of the contents. Some weeks ago we found a green slime coating the walls and having long since exhausted the purifying tablets bought in Corfu I've taken to dropping in a handful of small shingle each time just before refilling to scour the insides. Shaken around vigorously with a quart or so of water it comes out like pea soup but, as I remark to B. (who always seems to be watching at the wrong moment), 'Better out than in!'

We find also that *Lugworm*'s bilges must be swabbed with fresh water and dried completely at least once each week, for if the salt damp is allowed to lie there on the spare warps and rigging, they soon start to smell abominably. Today we have removed them all and are towing them astern to freshen up. The floorboards are piled on the foredeck meantime, and we've emptied all the lockers as well to give them an airing. Tins, packets, rigging, bedding and clothes are spread all over the boat; she looks like a Chinese funeral with we two strips of leather stretched out among the chaos. One wonders idly what would happen if a hurricane arrived out here halfway across the Tyrrhenian – maybe we'd see it coming, but life would be hectic for a while.

For want of something better to do I squint through the handbearing compass. The tip of Stromboli bears 274 degrees. What else is there to take a sight on? That faint grey pimple to the south-west must be Panarea – 248 degrees. It's not a good 'cut'; a bit too small an angle but it'll do, and the 'fix' puts us a sniff south of our trackline. Better alter course a couple of degrees and we should hit Vibo on the nose. I settle down comfortably with my back resting against the base of the mizzen mast, eyeing the flat steering compass strapped to the top of the centreboard casing and gradually become hypnotised by the blessed thing; but wait a minute! Isn't that something other than sea and sky fine over the starboard bow? A thin line of cloud, or land perhaps? I stand up to get higher, blink, and run my eyes slowly along, just above the horizon – it's the best way to pick out anything that isn't there.

'Stop wobbling the boat,' comes a sleepy voice from under the sampan hat, 'you'll upset the coffee.'

'I'm navigating!' I retort. A chap has to justify himself at times.

'Where are we,' she asks. 'Are we lost yet?'

B. has a peculiar approach to navigation. Unless she can say, with no shadow of doubt, that we're balanced exactly on the head of a pin in precisely THAT position – so far as she's concerned it's an emergency. She could be lost on Bodmin Moor on a fine day. For my part, as long as I know which ocean we're in, what matter? 'All right, cuckoo,' I mumble, 'we're somewhere between Stromboli and Italy, maybe a bit farther south than I thought but nothing to worry about.'

That does it.

The hat wobbles and two long brown legs unfold to start slithering about on the sloping hull bottom where the floor boards aren't. She tried to stand and sits down heavily again. A box of tools and a half full tin of varnish slide off the side-deck. The coffee is already in the bilges. I continue looking, steadfastly, towards Italy.

But it's no use; it's one of those hot days again and the pressure is high. I start thinking about ducks. Did you know they have a more or less airtight skull, and are prone to bouts of sudden flapping about and fits during summer thunderstorms? Something to do with rapid variation of atmospheric pressure on a small brain box.

Odd, because there's no thunder today.

'Where's the rag?' she says.

There's varnish, coffee and the tools all becoming intimate down there, but I stare unblinkingly towards Italy. 'The rag, quickly,' she squeaks, fossicking up under the side netting. My newly dhobeyed white jersey joins the sticky mess in the bilges.

'Oh God!' she shrieks, 'don't just stand up there like Eros, DO something!'

'Come back here, cuckoo,' I hiss, soothingly. 'Just take the helm and leave it to me. I'll clear up the mess and stow everything.'

She steps in it – then on to the chart. Honestly, sometimes I wonder if it wouldn't be simpler opting for the hurricane.

*   *   *

We never did make Vibo. Neither would you had you rounded Cape Zambrone and seen that crumbling golden ruin of the watchtower of Briatico and the gay fishing boats drawn up on the beach behind the tiny mole. It was a perfect little harbour half way along the carbuncle, just made for *Lugworm* to bury her nose in, and being about six in the evening we were ready for toast and honey and a refreshing swim to wash off the torpor of the day.

The fisherfolk were boisterously welcoming. We buried our anchor under the ample backside of Madonna di Pompeii and poodled around among the brilliant greens, golds and reds of Stella del Mare, Santa Gerardo and Rosa Madre, all bestrewn with nets, lines, buoys and boys, for each boat seemed to harbour its own small explosion of children.

'See!' One of the fishermen calls impatiently to us, 'FISH TV!' and he leaps aboard his boat to proudly uncover an expensive echo sounder, a trace of the sea-bed still faded and purple on the paper roll. 'Fish TV.' he grins again delightedly pointing to a faint shadow about twenty fathoms under the surface which may or may not have been a shoal. He is buoyant this one, and well he may be, for didn't he bring back two spendid tunny this morning, forty and sixty kilos each. So far as I can gather they'll reap a good harvest in lire if he's shrewd in the bargaining. 'And he'll have to be!' growls a companion, sotto voce as he mends his nets, 'to pay for that costly bit of nonsense – there's six months good eating mortgaged in that box.' A tinge of jealousy perhaps, but we wonder more and more at the economics of this fishing; we've been trailing a line now for more than six hundred miles and even the damned spinner complains of being lonely.

We wandered inland with the cool of the evening, up the dusty road and through the little village which lies about a kilometre from the harbour, resting our eyes on the green of the hills with their deeply wooded valleys which back the splendid sandy beaches. Northward round the Gulf of Eufemia we could see the coastline to be flatter, but about fifteen miles away beyond Cape Suvero it rose in a more continuous mountain range which sloped steeply to the sea. From the watch-tower it looked appealing.

And so it was. We set off on the morning of 5th June to skirt round the Gulf, using the lightest of westerly zephyrs until she, too, dropped off to sleep leaving us to anchor under the beautiful fortified headland town of Pizzo where we replenished our petrol supply. There was nothing for it but to motor gently on within feet of the beach, which became more and more shingly. By early evening, sated with sun and the blinding beach and sky, we were off the mouth of Fiume Amato and making a difficult entry against the strong outflow boiling over a shallow bar.

But it was well worth the effort, if only for the delight of bathing again in cool sweet fresh water. We washed all our clothes and spread them to dry on the pebbles, then walked inland along the deserted banks. Merely to use one's legs after hours in the boat is a delight. You cannot know the pleasure and contrast of wandering through reeds, bamboo, eucalyptus trees, grass and green scrub bushes after a day of blinding

BRIATICO

beach, sea and sky. To hear the sudden swift beat of a bird's wing, and glimpse the blue flash of a kingfisher as it darts along a leafy lane of green water. Breathing becomes a new delight, for there is always some fresh scent, a rich green breath of growing things, nourished by the river, and above all these is shadow – flickering pools of relief that come rustling with a million leafy voices bringing balm after the heat of day.

That night we cooked supper over a blazing log fire on the pebbles, listening to the quiet whisper of the sea, while a herd of oxen, attracted by the glow, ranged curiously back and forth on the opposite bank. But we slept aboard *Lugworm*, for the water and the tent deterred the insects, and somehow we always felt safer with a moat.

There remained more than five hundred miles of this Tyrrhenian coast before crossing the border up there into the French Riviera. The prevailing winds in this area are light north westerly, and every sailor knows that around the first or second week in August there is generally a period of violent weather. Our average of ten to twelve miles per day would see us in the region of Genoa by late July, and this was fine, for then we would be coasting along a weather shore which would offer the chance of a good lee from the northerly winds. But *Lugworm* bless her is not at her best beating to windward in light airs, particularly when heavily laden as she was, and we were quite prepared to motor much of the way.

I remember the next morning having ghosted round the lighthouse on Cape Suvero in a near calm, we passed through a shoal of dead tunny floating belly up on the surface. Large fish these, there were some fifty of them in varying stages of decomposition, and we never did unravel that mystery, for the flesh of this fish is highly prized. It may be that the long tunny nets – they stretched as much as six miles out from the shore – had simply caught too many fish for the boats to cope with, but it seemed unlikely. Yet death by pollution seemed even less likely so far south, for there was little heavy industry on this coast.

That was an interesting day's sail, some of it under power to fill in gaps between fitful gusts of wind. The hills, as we had expected, sloped quite steeply to the shore and a strange result of the many small mountain torrents was that during their brief winter cataract down the valleys they had over the years brought much rock and silt to build up a river bed which was actually higher than the surrounding low fringes of the beach. The road and railway which cling closely to this coast appeared therefore often to tunnel beneath these raised riverbeds: it was an odd sight and of course the rivers were now quite dry, but what happens when the winter torrents flow is anybody's guess; perhaps they were contained by man-made banks of shingle and rock for the last few hundred yards before plunging into the sea.

Late afternoon found us still south of Cape Bonifati and to our surprise – for it is unmarked as a harbour on our chart – the little coastal village of Cetraro proved to have a fine mole. It gave excellent protection from the north, west and east, but would not provide much peace when wind and sea came out of the south. Another good thing Cetraro gave us was the finest pizza we had throughout the whole of Italy, and I refer not only to the taste, but also to the sheer entertainment which accompanied its production, for I must tell you that the proprietor of the small and unostentatious Pizzeria just beyond the mole is an artist and a showman – and he knows it!

You may be acquainted with pizza, that popular round flat wedge of cooked pasta with its various highly seasoned fillings? It formed our staple diet, together with *spaghetti con pommodoro*, up the whole of this coast, for our bag of shekels, one year since leaving England, was becoming an embarrassment. Pizza and spaghetti is cheap. So also, thank God, is the local wine, and frankly we were both willing to forego the more attractive menus in exchange for the protracted freedom and adventure of our voyage. But join us for this memorable entertainment, sorrowing as you do so for that drear invention of the infra-red grill with its instant and expensive banishment of all flavour. Suffer instead a meal prepared and cooked entirely by hand, each ingredient of which is added, so it seems, by pure inspiration; for Guiseppe the proprietor, as I have said, is an artist.

He is also immensely large. Indeed, as he appears beaming from behind the raffia curtain his gaily striped apron advances like a spinnaker drawing full and gloriously on a dead run. One's heart, already warmed by the kindly, happy and totally wholesome giant, forgives the fact that the superbly flourished pasteboard menu contains but one item: Pizza Napolitana. The wine, in simple clarity, is local. But we spy a dish of anchovies among the clutter of utensils against the far wall.

We query the exact contents of the Pizza Napolitana, asking if these are included. 'But, of course,' beams Guiseppe clanking down a bottle of golden plonk and two thick glasses, 'and, Signore, you will be surprised!'

Against the back wall, which in fact is solid rock of the cliff face, a huge brick oven is built, and its wide mouth is glowing from a wood fire within. Guiseppe approaches this, looks inside at the inferno, and begins to sing. His voice is quite simply magnificent – how could it be otherwise, born in that great barrel chest? Indeed, it is the sort of voice that in sheer quality of tone and power, spurns instrumental accompaniment. He sings a popular Italian ballad with pure joy, and as he does so takes up an iron-handled rake, plunges it deep in the oven and withdraws Hades – spitting, flaming and astonished – out on to the stone floor where, to the accompaniment of a victorious crescendo, it is banished sizzling to a damp corner.

A galvanised bucket stands to one side of the oven. Into this he dips a massive hand to withdraw a dripping rag which is pulled expertly through the closed circle of his forefinger and thumb to remove excess water, and then with practised skill he knots one corner of it to the end of the rake handle. 'It is good – the wine?' he beams, and ashamed we realise we have not yet poured ourselves a drink, for the show has been too enthralling. Guiseppe bears down on us reproachfully and fills our two glasses then pours himself another and together we take the first portentous mouthful. *'Salute!'* he carols, rolling the liquid around in his cheeks. 'Ah … but is it not like the milk of the Madonna herself?' With this benign giant standing there, so open-heartedly, so very sincerely waiting for our approval – it is.

He returns to the oven, humming with a deep rich satisfied rumble and takes up the rake with the wet rag attached. Then begins a truly masterly piece of syncopation. The long handle of the rake, endowed now with all the magic of a conductor's baton, is coaxed back and forth, in and out, and the spitting hissing rag rolls itself into a rope and begins to revolve like a Catherine wheel over the circular brick floor. Ashes spin to the walls as this steaming centrifuge first sweeps, then washes, and finally burnishes the cauterised bricks. Startled gouts of steam, matched cloud for cloud by swelling volumes of song spurt from the door to escape thankfully up through the rattan roof; and Guiseppe is obviously happy.

There is a large enamel bowl of the pasta ready mixed to hand, and adjacent are smaller dishes, the contents of which are not yet clear. He flicks a sprinkle of water on to the now dark oven floor, listens to the instant vaporisation with practised ear, and nods approvingly. The oven is ready.

I have seen my mother rolling pastry and kneading dough for bread, and marvelled at her skill. But I have never, nor ever shall again, watch such a miracle of dexterity as now took place. The pasta – one almost hears its sigh of resignation – is withdrawn in one lightning swoop from the basin, and quicker than eye can follow flattens of its own volition on the cold marble slab alongside. Then two great hands – living embodiment of those cataracts of sonic joy – imbue that limp pancake with a life of its own. It rises, apparently inspired by the mere proximity of those fingers, and spins in the air like a conjuror's plate to drop, surely destined for the ashy floor, only to stop in mid air, fold itself neatly in two halves and flatten once more on the slab where some – to us undetected – imperfection is already liquidated in a fresh and waiting embryo. We watch those hands, hypnotised, and so catch the quick glance from his happy eyes, the glance of a master who knows he is perfect and has totally captured his audience.

With a fresh outburst of song the favoured cake, crimped now at the edges and circular without flaw finds itself on the blade of a broad wooden shovel. A flick of the wrist and Guiseppe sprinkles its astonished face with chopped tomatoes. *'Tommodori,'* he roars between stanzas and then, in neat order and each accompanied by its own appropriate grimace, *'Mozzarella, olive, cipolle,'* and on went a spluther of finely chopped onions. Capers, black pepper and garlic followed and then, with a dreamy expression accompanied by ecstatic sniffs, *'Origani sulla montagna!'*

And finally, *'Oho!'* he shouts, *'Tacciuga,* much anchovy, eh? And more, for the smile of the Signora!' as another shower of the salty fishes flushes the startled pizza, to be followed by olive oil, liberally sprinkled from a watering can – and into the oven it goes.

Guiseppe turns, raising his hands in a gesture of feigned horror. *'Signore!* But ... the wine!' And sure enough, the bottle in some miraculous fashion has become empty. It is a moment only for another to take its place and with it comes Guiseppe to sit with us, bringing added warmth to a world that is already glowing round the edges. 'And that is your tiny boat there?' he asks, pointing to *Lugworm* who is still visible in the dusk. We tell him our story and he listens, his fluid face registering astonishment, incredulity, disbelief, and then softly, his eyes wide with genuine wonder, 'but such happiness! To sail our lovely coast in such a boat, the two of you alone like … like … the Odyssey!'

There is a rich scent of roasting anchovies. The giant rises, takes the wooden shovel and slides it neatly under the bubbling pizza. He draws it towards him, gives it a quick twist and once more it is lying dead-centre in the oven. No trace of ash nor charred splinter of the pungent sweet smelling wood flaws its browning crust, but it is not quite ready and Guiseppe lights two candles and places them on our table. He stands then for a while looking down at B. 'The Signora's hair,' he says at last, 'I have been looking … you do not mind? It is like a Mass!' I glanced across to where the candlelight is catching her blonde curls. They seem to glow as though returning something of the sun's radiance that has soaked into them all day, and I look at him more closely, this gentle giant; he has a strange turn of phrase. A Mass!

But the pizza is ready – and we are more than ready for it. Guiseppe retires behind the raffia curtain as we savour every mouthful washed down with more 'Milk of the Madonna Herself'. And there are still some five hundred miles of this enchanted coast, and then all the canals of France, and the whole summer lies before us. Lucky, lucky us!

Maybe if we had to choose one memory only from this strange quixotic experience called life – one memory to last the whole of eternity – well, perhaps that night at Cetraro would be our choice.

We were content.

*　　*　　*

Yes, as we slowly worked our way up that coast it was easy to imagine ourselves by some strange alchemy transposed in time from the legendary days of Ulysses. Acciaroli, which you will not find on the map for it is a mere oversight of the coast scarce large enough to protect its own small fishing boats, opened its sleepy eye one evening to see *Lugworm* nosing into its narrow entrance and kindly bared a few feet of its dusty beach to accommodate this stranger from the sea. And even as she was drawn up, aided by the hoary old fishermen, to nestle between her tarry smelling sisters, the sky became black and overcast and that well-known brooding calm enveloped us, forewarning of the inevitable storm. Watched in silent amazement we rigged the tent and it was during the next blustery three days, pinned on that beach, that we became entranced with the place, and largely through the medium of a window.

You might not think that a window could capture the imagination and hold one spellbound, but that is because you have not laid as we did hour after hour under *Lugworm*'s tent listening to the searing breath of a gale that came hounding up from the south – with nothing but that window high in the crumbling wall above the harbour peering down at us, a square black hole with peeling green shutters glowering in through our turned-back flap. It was there in the morning, gazing over the harbour and beyond to the distant sea, and it was there in the night, a flickering square of golden light until the eyelid shutters closed, but never face nor form did we see giving soul to the eye. No, I doubt whether you would find another window such as that if you searched the whole world, for what other window is there which peers across the harbour mole where the gale-blown swell fumes and bursts in a storm of driven white, filling the uneasy boats with weed and grit, lifting the dust and sand from the beach and blasting the tight-shut doors with its breath of utter disdain.

And then, from that window, when the storm has eased one might hear the drone of the bent old forms mending their nets down below, and the account of how there had been so many tunny that scores of them had to be left, for the boats could not hold more with safety. So last week, under the Torre Guardia down Diamonte way, the stink of the blown fish cleared the village for a whole day until they sent for a boat to tow the carcasses to sea again. But at night from behind that casement, when the voices from the Albergo drone and lift in a murmur of argument, that eye in the old cracked wall looks at the church across the piazza aglow in the ochre light of the street lamp, and braces itself as it watches the great bell in the campanile begin to swing even before it roars out to the drowsy paese its rolling reminder of the evergone moment, echoing across the listening sea to where those brilliant beads of light dip and twinkle on the horizon, and the women of the village watch, and hope.

No, you may find many another window in many another crumbling wall, but this window knows Acciaroli, and we have known it too.

The weather grew calm again and we slowly worked our way up towards the Gulf of Salerno. One hot afternoon, happening on a small cluster of houses at the waterside we witnessed, amid great excitement, the landing of a large tunny. It must have weighed some three hundred kilo for the boat, unable to pull the fish aboard, was obliged to tow it to a small jetty. There it was with difficulty hoisted by block and tackle to be gutted on a mobile dray, bespattering the jetty and many of the excited onlookers with blood. *'Presto! Presto!'* shouted an impatient fisherman as I clambered atop a pile of boxes to get my picture and then, laughingly, I was offered the entire severed head, its open mouth and staring eyes a picture of astonishment.

Shortly after, nosing alongside an early morning mist which lay thick over the low-lying shore, we dropped anchor and

landed to stretch our legs along a dusty track which led directly inland through the woods. A ruined wall of gigantic stone
blocks soon appeared to our left, and scrabbling with the liz-
ards we climbed this to look across what, five hundred years
before Christ, had been the precincts of Paestum, that religious
centre whose remains today contain nothing but three Doric
temples. But in their magnificent isolation these are claimed
to be the most perfect Doric temples in existence. Looking at
them that morning, before the last of the mist had dispersed
and before even the first of the tourists had arrived, we believed the claim, and just stood and gazed in silent awe – until a
movement in the grass at our feet revealed a thick black snake,
coiled and surveying the two of us in anything but silent awe.
We removed ourselves, pondering the fact that this entire city
which was once a great trading port should have been so completely deserted by the sea.

It was the fifteenth of June when, seeking to refresh ourselves again in river water, we surfed into the Fiume Sele to
the south of Salerno; it might have been better had we not.
We swam and washed ourselves just inside the river mouth
on a deserted pebbly beach flanked by tall pampas grasses,
and then emptied *Lugworm* entirely, washing out her lockers and the bilges. All our gear was spread about the beach
to air, and evening was coming on before everything was
re-stowed. There seemed no point in carrying on up towards
Salerno that day; indeed we preferred the peace of this lovely
river to the bustle of a busy harbour. So thinking to break
the spell that decreed we catch not a single fish, we set off up
river under sail, steering with a stern oar for fear of damaging the rudder on any shoals or under water obstructions. It
was a still calm evening, and I remember as we ran silently
under mainsail alone up the huge green river, being startled

140

at what appeared to be a section of the surface suddenly lifting skywards.

It turned out to be a colossal fine-meshed net all of sixty feet square which, by a clever arrangement of poles and pulleys, could be lowered horizontally down to the river bed and hoisted at a moment's notice by means of two taut overhead wires. There was no sign of any fishermen, and so intrigued were we with the mechanism of the thing that we quite forgot that the top of our gaff was some eighteen inches higher than the sagging centre of the net.

Lugworm was brought-up all standing, pinned by the top of her mast until with a twang like a snapping banjo wire the main halyard parted to bring gaff and sail crashing down. The effect ashore was alarming. A group of vociferous Italians exploded from the bushes, gesticulating wildly and leaving us in no doubt that the cause of their concern was only that madly swinging net and certainly not our own fate. Luckily there was no real damage on either hand, and concern rapidly turned to laughter as we closed the bank to pour oil on troubled waters.

We saw many more instances of these 'skyhook nets' as we came to call them and it is worth describing them in more detail. Two poles of wood or metal are erected about seventy feet apart on both banks, each pair opposite the other. Being in the region of thirty feet tall this calls for a deal of complicated rigging, and through the blocks at the top of one pair two stout wires are rove, led across the river, and secured to the top of the opposite poles. The running end of these wires is then led down to a windlass which has to be firmly anchored to stand the considerable strain, and this windlass is sometimes hand operated or it may be driven by a small electric motor. By bringing the two wires down to each end of the same windlass drum, easing out on both wires will automatically ensure that they sag at an exactly equal rate into the river. The net is then attached by two of its sides to the wires about halfway across the river, and from its centre hangs a short umbilical cord, knotted at the lower end.

You will appreciate that the span of the wires can be as much as three hundred yards, and the net (large though it is) takes up only a small section of the middle of them so that when the windlass is eased off, the resultant curve is not very great out there halfway across the river. Down sinks the net to rest on the river bed. No bait appears to be used, but every fifteen minutes or so a quick turn of the windlass and up it shoots bringing with it anything which might have been floating or swimming above it. We saw one fine fish plucked from its element wiggling madly up there in the net and working itself down to the centre as it did so. A small rowing boat was immediately despatched from shore and by the time it was beneath the net, that fish had obligingly worked itself down into the umbilical cord. The rower simply undid the knot and the fish fell into the boat. We saw modifications of this type of net rigged out on ridiculous overhead gantries from clifftops, piers and beaches as we worked northward, and it was evident that fish formed a valuable part of the local diet. It never did ours.

That night we anchored about four miles up the Sele river and it was next morning that disaster struck. I must explain that our usual method of leaving these rivers was under power, so as to shorten that tricky moment of crossing the bar with its attendant breakers. We would therefore leave the rudder unshipped, have the centreplate hoisted, and steer with the outboard. Remember it was necessary to watch carefully before heading over the bar, for the waves nearly always occur in cycles of large, then small, and it's important to go through them when they're small. Of course, the whole procedure is much faster when making an exit, for then one has the strength of the outflow working with one, not to mention the safety factor of the boat's bow being presented to the seas rather than her stern which is the case when entering.

An onshore wind had developed during the night bringing a bit of a sea with it, and this was breaking three or four lines deep all along the width of the bar. We poodled around just inside the mouth, choosing the right moment, and then set off to pass smartly through the breakers. It was not until we were through and I had set mizzen and jib, lowered the centreplate and moved back to ship the rudder that we became aware that there was no rudder to ship. Can you imagine it? We looked at each other, appalled, and slowly the fact became clear: we had sailed and motored the boat four miles up and four miles down that festering river, fished unsuccessfully, slept aboard – and not once in all that time had either of us twigged the fact that I had left the rudder on that beach when cleaning out the boat.

Well, there was nothing for it; back into the river it had to be. But this was quite another matter for now we would have to present the boat's stern to the breakers and be working against that strong outflow. I looked at the exposed beach and all hope of landing there faded immediately – the waves were too big. So we waited outside the bar for the critical moment, and then with the engine full throttle headed in again. This time we were not quite so lucky. The outflow was slowing our speed over the bottom to little more than half a knot and the time we took to move through the danger area was sufficient for another series of large waves to overtake us. I could see them building up astern, and it's not conducive to peace of mind, believe me, when you watch them shortening up, rearing, and then just as they reach the boat, crashing over with a roar. Realising we were going to be caught right in the thick of them, I yelled to

B. to hold on tight and kept *Lugworm's* stern true into the line of breakers. As the first hill of water crept upon us she cocked her stern up, lunged forward at a terrifying pace, then balanced for a moment on the crest and slid down the back just as the wave broke ahead of her. But not so with the second wave; this broke just astern.

Oh crumbs; anyone who knows the way of a boat held in the grip of a wave will know that ghastly feeling as she lifts aft to remain poised in the jaws of that creaming line of foam. *Lugworm* was surfing. In a crazy minute of wild uncontrol she lunged in on the advancing face of that breaker, and Heaven alone knows how she didn't broach – it was certainly nothing to do with me, for remember I had no rudder. One can only assume that the skeg of the outboard was sufficient to hold the stern into the seas, for we were going twice as fast as that engine ever achieved. Yes, it was quite a moment but *Lugworm* made it and while B. bailed out the water which had squirted up through the outboard well, I scanned the beach hopefully for the rudder. I knew exactly where I had laid it on the pebbles – but it was no longer there.

This was a serious blow. 'Drascombe Lugger rudders,' I remarked to B. as we closed the beach to start searching and think things out, 'are very sophisticated bits of equipment, not to be lightly "knocked up" from a few bits and pieces.' No; this was a real disaster. I couldn't see us sailing another fifteen hundred miles or so using an oar to steer, yet at the same time the complexities of having a complete unit despatched from the builders to some forgotten outpost of the Tyrrhenian seaboard made one feel weak. 'We've just GOT to find it, even if we have to cause an International Situation; and who the blazes could want to pinch a useless bit of equipment like that?' I fumed.

'Brass,' she answered, and of course that was it: the top hinged fitting on the tiller was solid brass and worth a small fortune to a scrap dealer.

You may be sure we searched the banks, waded out into the fast flowing current (thinking children might have thrown it into the water), and finally in desperation combed the pampas woods, but to no avail. So finally we spent the whole of next day locating a policeman and the proprietor of a farmstead we found back in the hinterland – and I leave you to imagine the hopelessness of trying to describe our loss, we who didn't even know the Italian for 'rudder'. By the following evening it was quite clear that it was gone for good, and somehow we had to get a replacement made. Obviously, Salerno some fifteen miles up the coast was the best hope, so we sailed there next day, steering with the oar, and great fun it was before a brisk quartering wind, but to tell the truth we were somewhat downcast, for that tiller had been fashioned for us by a good friend in Greece after an episode in the Saronic Gulf, and it was rather like losing a limb of *Lugworm*, entirely through our own negligence.

*   *   *

Our approach to Salerno was somewhat daunting. It is a large and flourishing harbour imbued with that sense of hectic bustle which characterises most Italian seaports, and we were a little overawed by such activity. But in a situation like this, I'm a firm believer in going right to the top and working down through the hierarchy of authority to the chap who is actually going to get on with the job. A replacement had to be obtained. It was a complicated bit of mechanism for which there would be no template available. Only I knew exactly what was needed. We would therefore sail right into the biggest yacht club present – if any – and ask for the Commodore.

We did.

The *Circolo Canottieri Irno*, or as we would say the Irno Yacht Club of Salerno, is a splendidly active, crowded and sophisticated establishment jammed between the busy Via Porto and the sea, flanked by the arms of the Molo Manfredi and the Molo Gennaio. Its floating pontoons are crammed with large racing dinghies, fast runabouts and elegant cruisers. It does not really cater for visitors, being hard put to find room for its own members' boats. We sailed into the thick of them, spotted one slot conspicuous by its emptiness, and tied up. Our Red Ensign flying from the truck of the mizzen drew polite attention, and in response to a query from an adjacent yacht I asked if the Commodore might perhaps be available for a word? I was led into a building on the quayside, up a dark cool flight of stairs, past some offices and on to a large roofed balcony overlooking the yacht harbour. It was cool, altogether pleasant, and there was a very active bar. Eventually a large gentleman in a white shirt and grey flannels, followed by a retinue of what I assume were club officers came forward. 'Signor Capone, Presidente di Club Irno,' he said, extending his hand. 'Can I be of any help?' Through an interpreter I explained my predicament, and the need to employ an intelligent metalworker, preferably from a boatyard, to produce under my direction as near a replica of the lost unit as possible.

Signor Capone walked to the edge of the balcony and surveyed the crowded boats below. 'Which is your yacht?' he asked. 'There,' I pointed, adding 'actually you cannot see her at the moment, she's behind that Flying Fifteen.' The group peered down to where the two masts of our dinghy showed above the other boat's hull, then the President looked at his fellow officers and again at me. 'Let us go and examine your boat,' he smiled, and together we all proceeded back down the pontoon. I introduced him to B. who, looking totally gorgeous in her wide straw hat and a flowered shimmery sort of vest – she might just have stepped from the Isis after a morning's punting – smiled appealingly and apologised for the trouble we were causing. 'It is OUR pleasure, Signora,' the President replied, offering his hand as she disembarked, and then, turning to me, asked, 'And where, Captain, have you come from?'

'Greece,' I said. 'We are sailing to England.'

There was a moment of evident perplexity and then, as though all had suddenly become clear, he exclaimed 'Ah, I did not understand. This is your tender. Your yacht then is perhaps at anchor outside?' and everyone peered out to sea as though looking for signs of a funnel or masts.

'No, Signor President,' I replied through the interpreter. 'This is our yacht. She is called *Lugworm* and is a very noble stouthearted boat and is taking us to England – if we can get her a new rudder.'

There was an incredulous murmuring among the group, and suddenly the whole atmosphere changed. Away went the slightly formal approach, the polite but distant hospitality. In its place came interest, curiosity, and informal good natured questioning. Jackets and shoes were removed while members boarded *Lugworm* to be introduced to Foogoo. I explained our commodious living quarters, the staterooms either side the centreboard casing, the private wardrobes and the separate engine room. I showed them the marquee which we rigged at night, and word meanwhile had flown far and wide, so that our pontoon became quite unstable with more and more interested members. Finally Signor Capone (relative, we were jokingly assured, of the infamous Al) having held consultation with his officers, announced that from that moment on we were honorary members, that the entire facilities of the Club

147

were at our disposal for just as long as we needed them, and that the member who spoke fluent English would gladly conduct me to a 'man who matters' who would know exactly how to manufacture a new rudder and tiller. Meanwhile would the Signora and myself not join them on the balcony for a drink, where we would be presented with the Club Burgee? In the meantime the club crane would be prepared for lifting our 'yacht' from the water in order that vital measurements might be taken.

It was all rather overwhelming, after the weeks of roughing it up rivers and behind rocks, constantly on the alert for hazards from a dozen different quarters, to find ourselves most hospitably sunk in settees knocking back the cooling drinks while under our feet, the astonished *Lugworm* was already dangling high above the water, encircled by two stout slings, while workmen danced attendance rigging chocks on the quayside to hold her ample belly.

Overwhelming perhaps, but it was a very real relief to know ourselves among sailors and friends who, in a metaphorical if not literal sense 'spoke our language', felt for our predicament, and were openly and genuinely prepared to give every possible help.

Meanwhile I was asked to make an accurate drawing of the lost rudder, which I produced instantly, having thought of little else since the awful discovery. In company with our good friend the interpreter I was conducted out of the club, up some broad steps on to the busy Via Porto where, at risk of our lives, we dodged the onslaught of traffic. We plunged from the blinding light into the dim cavern of a warehouse and our ears flinched before the shriek of metal in torment.

The 'man who mattered' turned out to be a small gentleman of some forty years of age, with a sallow face, blue chin, oily

148

hands and dressed in a grey overall. While the interpreter explained the situation my eyes grew accustomed to the darkness
and I looked round the metal shop. It was obviously part of a
ship builders' premises and my heart lifted as I spied, in a far
corner, scores of gleaming steel rods. They looked just about
the right size for *Lugworm*'s rudder post, and that, I knew, was
going to be the stumbling block if there was one; metal plate
was always for the having, and for that matter I could make
the tiller myself; it was the post and the welding and the metal cutting which was beyond us. My drawing was examined.
Our friend from the Club explained the technical details and
in company with a young apprentice we all four trooped back
to *Lugworm* for further discussion. Returning back across the
Via Porto the 'gentleman who mattered' stopped in his tracks,
caught hold of my arm, and in a conspiratorial whisper hissed:
'Urgente?' I looked at him and weighed up the situation. *'Molto
urgente!'* I replied, looking just as rich as I dared.

'Domani!' he said, and we parted.

I shall never forget that *'domani'*. The apprentice, a power-
fully built blond-haired youth with brilliant blue eyes, had
been placed in total charge of the job, told to get on with it, do
anything I asked and make it snappy. We started at eight. By
eight-thirty we had made the discovery that my rudder trunking diameter was not of any standard size. By nine o'clock we
were carrying a fifteen foot length of solid twenty-seven mil-
limetre diameter steel rod across the Via Porto, to the strident
anguish of a queue of lorries and other traffic. By nine twenty
we were carrying it back again, it was a millionth of a something too thick, and the morning was growing hot. The apprentice thereupon wanted to start cutting into a 24 mm rod
but I'm a great believer in what is called 'offering it up' first, and
so for a third time the traffic in the Via Porto ground to a noisy

halt, while that incredibly heavy rod was manhandled over to *Lugworm*, and since the rods were preserved in a thick coating of axle grease, the day was becoming sticky, to say nothing of *Lugworm*'s after deck.

But the rod was too thin; it rattled loosely in the trunking and would drive us mad when sailing. Somewhere, it was clear, we had to get a bit of 26 mm rod, but the apprentice was looking glum. Once again we stopped the traffic, and then all work in the factory too while the foreman, the 'gentleman who mattered' and half the employees searched for that odd piece which had been left over from ... you know the bit ... surely that was 26 mm in diameter? Eventually it was unearthed from behind a pile of metal plate and the calipers applied. It was 25 mm. It also had half a ship welded on to the other end.

Again the traffic ground to a halt while the contraption, reduced in size but still awkward and very heavy was manoeuvred across, down through the Club, along the pontoon and aboard *Lugworm*. The rod was loose, but for want of better it would have to do. By now it was late morning and I was learning that the south-facing quays and highways of Industrial Salerno bear an all too close affinity with Inferno. We were both running with sweat and caked in grease. As a precaution B. had disappeared with our fast dwindling Traveller's Cheques to find a bank. By noon the blade was cut, shaped, and welded to the post. By mid afternoon the complicated hinged tiller head with retaining collar was completed and also welded to the top of the post, and a very clever engineering job it all was too. But it didn't fit the rudder trunking. The welding between blade and post, stood proud and prevented the blade slotting down between the trunking plates. By teatime the apprentice and I had a deep and mutual admiration for each other's determination. The weld was ground off, other adjustments made, and

… Eureka! The rudder sank down through that narrow slot. But it would not turn. The distance between that top collar and the highest point of the blade was a micro-something or other short, and it jammed. Yet again we cavorted up to the factory where I observed, a little apprehensively, that all the workers were preparing to leave. 'You …' and I looked at the apprentice with despair in my heart, for I was determined to get that rudder finished on one day … 'You – go?'

'Marbor,' he replied.

Marbore? Marbo? What the devil did he mean?

'Zigarette Marbor,' he enlightened me, and whistled softly as he doodled with his finger on a dusty oil drum top. I'd never heard of the brand, but scuttled off to find a tobacconist's shop. *'Zigarette Marbor,'* I gasped, having tracked one down in the town.

'Marbor?' exclaimed the tobacconist, looking blank.

'Marbo … Marboi … Malbo …' Desperately I tried all inflexions in an attempt to reproduce the sound, scanning the shelves the while. There were Players, Philip Morris, Gitanes, Nationale and Marlboro … . MARLBORO!

'Marlboro,' I exclaimed, pointing to the red and gold packets.

'Si, si … Marbo,' replied the proprietor, and of course, they were quite the most expensive in the shop. Frantically I scuttled back along the Via Mercanti, down the Lungomare Trieste and into the Via Porto to surprise the apprentice who hastily slipped a packet of Nationale into his back pocket, while holding out his hand for the six packets of Marlboro. Negotiations were resumed. The 'gentleman who mattered' surveyed the situation also, looked pointedly at his watch, accepted the two packets of Marlboro with thanks and disappeared back into the now silent factory muttering 'Molto Urgente!'

The blade was ground down a thou or so and once more we wore that groove back to *Lugworm*. B. was back aboard cleaning up the mess. 'Cuckoo,' I said, feeling a bit faint, 'I think we're very nearly home and dry!' She looked at the rusty blade with the carbon-crusted weld, the great iron collar on the top, and the heavy bolt and nut which protruded from one side, and said 'Strewth!' Which could have meant anything.

'Have you got the cash?' I asked her.

She had. I bought a pot of grey paint and weakly sat down for a trifling financial calculation with the 'gentleman who mattered'. I left feeling positively limp, but the job was done. Crude maybe, but it worked and we could sail again.

'One thing troubles me,' said B. early the following morning as I penned an appreciative letter to the President of the Club 'what happens if we bend THIS rudderpost – we can't drop it through the bottom of the boat like the other one; that top collar is welded on.'

'There's only one possible answer to that,' I replied. 'This one we JUST DON'T BEND!' And we motored past the end of the mole and set course for Capri.

*   *   *

Capri was both magnificent and horrific. We circumnavigated the island, marvelling at the awe-inspiring cliffs, the wooded ravines and miraculously beautiful bays, keeping the while a cautious distance from the throbbing beaches and jostling tripper boats. No glimpse could be gained of the entrance to the famous Blue Grotto for a fleet of hire boats swarming there. B. dodged ashore for some urgently needed provisions while I remained with the boat, standing off into deep water to escape the hordes of clamouring swimmers who threatened to swamp her by their sheer numbers.

Lugworm distinguished herself by sailing through the *Sotto-passaggio di Mezzo* – a colossal natural arch through the rocks off Punta Tragara – only to escape annihilation by the bloom on her topsides from a thirty-knot gin palace with similar but reciprocal intent.

We were glad to leave. These middle latitudes of Italy's western seaboard are incredibly beautiful but, as B. sadly pointed out, 'There are just too many of us; we're annihilating the very thing we come for.'

It was near the end of June that we found the delightful little port of Sperlonga, unmarked as such on our chart, and since the small harbour was jam packed with pleasure craft we anchored outside just east of the new mole. We spent three days wandering round the streets of this lovely headland village and here too, one hot morning after coffee in the piazza high in the fortified village that, as was my custom, I casually made my way to a vantage point from which, far below, I could see *Lugworm* and check that all was well.

I looked, and blinked. She was bristling with small children. They were crawling in under her tent, diving off her bow, and walking the slippery pole of her boomkin. I could see one of them through my binoculars attempting to wrench off the lock of the forward hatch, aft another was busy rifling the netting shelves. I handed the glasses to B. and set off down the zigzag path from the citadel faster, I'll warrant, than anyone before or since. I feared mightily for the boomkin, which was never intended to be used as a diving board, being but a pliant spar. But my approach, hot-foot and flying, had not gone unnoticed; those ever watchful eyes twigged me before I so much as got to the beach – and overboard they all went, like a slippery shoal of fishes, swimming madly to the end of the mole. I caught them – it was a tactical error on their part for I now commanded the only escape route since they could not remain swimming around for ever. Maybe they did not expect a visiting boat's captain to break the four minute mile and still have fight left afterwards, but it was a very sorry band of ragamuffins that eventually faced me, cornered. One of them was bleeding profusely from his foot. I approached slowly, looking as fierce as possible, trying not to laugh at the dejected band and then, with a roar that I swear could be heard back up in Sperlonga bellowed, 'Va via!' aiming a feigned kick at the backside of the largest. They went.

Lugworm was in chaos. Blood was spattered over the decks and gear, our clothing strewn about. Obviously they had been after two things: cigarettes and money. Since we were both non-smokers and broke, they chose badly, but it served to make us more wary in future. Hitherto, throughout Greece and the extreme south of Italy, we had no qualms about leaving the boat and gear. But now, approaching the more populous and affluent metropolitan areas, the usual lowering of standards was becoming evident.

Indeed, a subtle change was taking place in our attitude towards the cruise. We found, alas, as we crept northwards, that we were no longer hungering to know what lay round the next headland, nor looking forward to landing on deserted beaches to explore a wild and barren hinterland. We began to talk with nostalgia of days spent beachcombing and sitting round driftwood fires alone and at peace long into the night. Indeed we now knew only too well, as we picked our way through growing flotillas of luxury cruisers and floating gin-dens EXACTLY what lay round the next bend and behind those immaculately raked beaches with their ranks of sun brollies and their 'NO LANDING' notices. And I will pass the opinion now that if mankind had conspired to kill stone dead any last vestige of sea-fever in his soul, he could not have devised a more effective means than his invention of the marina.

Neptune preserve me from the mass development of mass facilities for mass sailors. We were to slot on occasions into those vast and jam-packed soulless parking lots in Northern Italy and along the French Riviera – and paid handsomely for the privilege. But the supermarkets and plush restaurants at the end of the pontoons, and the casinos and knick-knackery shops close ashore and the whole way of life of a large proportion of the populace began to awaken old base desires. We were in danger of growing effete and tired of life and even began to view the sea with a patronising air. Oh Heaven forbid!

Until one day when casting about in the bilges, I came across a letter from my Bank Manager and I don't know which frightened me more; that or the deplorable state of affairs into which we were in danger of sinking. There was only one remedy for both; to get to sea immediately and to stay there as long as possible.

But even that now had its additional hazards. It was, I remember, on the glorious fourth of July that, after a short stay at the marina on Cape Circeo just south of Anzio, we were ghosting in baking heat before a very light land-breeze some hundred yards seaward of the Pontine Marshes. The beaches here are formed of low-lying sandy dunes with occasional ducts into the lakes behind, all of which are inaccessible from the sea, and four hours of blistering heat was beginning to take its effect. For a pleasant respite just south of a small headland we anchored and took a swim. A crumbling Roman viaduct which must have originally carried the road to the ruined Torre Astura on the point, lay behind us, and we spent an hour or so exploring the submerged traces of houses and fortifications around the foot of the tower before gently idling on under the outboard, for all vestiges of wind had died.

We were both in a very soporific state when B. gave a small gasp and sat bolt upright. 'Did you see that?' she hiccupped pointing seaward. 'Over there. It must have been a large fish jumping, there was a tremendous splash and a spout of water shot upwards!'

'LOOK,' she squeaked, 'there's another.'

I stopped the engine, since its noise prevented us hearing anything far off. Sure enough, my eye caught the end of a shower of spray about half a mile seaward of us, but there was no sign of a fish, nor any sound.

Together we stood peering about in a silent world of baking heat under that sultry sky, listening and looking, for there was something strangely alarming about those spouts of water.

Then we both heard an unearthly throbbing whistle, and I felt the bristles on my neck quivering. Anyone who has ever heard shells whining overhead will know the sound, for that is precisely what it was, and some two hundred yards on the bow another shower of water shot skywards with a staccato 'slap'.

'B.,' I said, hastily pulling on my shorts, 'we're being shelled!' There didn't seem to be much point in trying to conceal the fact, since another howling banshee was lobbing noisily across.

'Shelled!' she gasped. 'Don't be ridiculous, who would want to shell US? We're not at war are we – well not with Italy, surely? Oh, no, it's just ridiculous. Anyway, they aren't exploding are they?'

It was true. Apart from the whine of their trajectory as they zoomed past, there was no other sound, but this, as I pointed out, was rather academic; I didn't think it would make a lot of difference if one of them actually hit us, and told her so.

We were about half a mile offshore and with the glasses I scanned the coast. About a mile back there was a tall white tower with what looked like a large water tank atop, and from above this I could just see a limp red flag drooping. I ranged the glasses along the coast and there, about a mile ahead was another. In between the two were a succession of squares, some twenty or so feet in height and made apparently of solid concrete. But they were in horrifying stages of disruption, with jagged ends of reinforced steel strands sticking out like hairs on end. Quite clearly, we were poodling around slap in the middle of a firing range, and what was more, the heavy artillery either didn't know or just didn't care. There was no sign of any boat, and we were alone on a sea calm as a millpond, except for those goosepimpling splashes.

'Well, what do we DO?' squeaked B., as another banshee zoomed past, and it was a good question.

There were four simple choices. We could either turn back, go on, go straight out to sea, or beach immediately. I looked at the beach. The thought of landing at the foot of those gruesome tombstones was horrifying. If we puttered out to sea at our full four knots we would simply ensure that we remained squarely in the danger area for at least another hour; and even then a freak overshoot could quite possibly send us to the bottom just beyond the horizon in splendid isolation. No: we either went back or went on, as fast as possible.

Since the risk was equal which ever we did, it was logical to go on, but at the exact moment I gave a tug at the outboard starter cord the air above and around us exploded. I cannot otherwise describe the sheer stunning 'crack' of that sound; it were as though the noise came from within one's own head instead of outside. B. shrieked, and I sat down dazed, holding my ears, wondering if perhaps we had suffered a direct hit and were already dead. Nothing happened. There was no sign of a shellburst, no gout of water, no smoke even in the sky, nothing. Just the ringing echo of that tremendous sonic 'crash'. It was quite ghastly.

'What on earth ...' came B.'s frightened voice and together we again took stock of the situation.

Another gout of water shot skywards dead astern. That did it. With the outboard at full throttle we nosed on, eyes glued to those horrible squares on shore. Twice more we nearly jumped from our skins as the electrifying blast shattered our ears, but no aerial nor subterranean explosions took place, nor was there any sign of hits scored on the targets.

I can only conclude that there was some form of beamed warning sound system meant to attract the attention of boats which strayed into the danger zone, but how this was effected remains a mystery. Suffice it to say that, a quarter of an hour later, and well clear of the second white tower, a highspeed military launch came speeding towards us. On its foredeck stood a portly Italian officer – whether he was Army or Navy was difficult to tell, for he wore grey uniform trousers and a white shirt rolled to the elbows. It drew impressively alongside and the large gentleman, who was obviously very hot and appeared to be not quite recovered from his siesta leaned importantly over the rails and pointed back to the firing range.

'No' he said wagging his finger admonishingly. No, no ... you not go there!'

'No, Signore,' I answered him, with equal authority. 'We not go there ... we come!'

This seemed to take him aback somewhat. He looked us over for a while, and then his face broke into a smile. 'Yes?' He beamed holding back a chuckle. 'I see. You come, that VERY good!' And he was still roaring with laughter as the powerful launch purred into life and swept effortlessly off.

Well, it was one way of looking at it.

*   *   *

By mid July we were in Elba, spending far too much time snorkelling underwater to examine the rocky bottom for non-existent fish, and by now were quite accustomed to being an object of open curiosity as we had worked our way up past the entrance to the Tiber, past endless populous beaches and lidos. Fleets of twin-hulled pedallos would come out when the weather was suitable, to pedal alongside until the lusty occupants tired. Huge tripping boats, painted a riotous camouflage of colours and crammed with camera-wielding holiday-makers, throbbed from the beaches and circled us. It was becoming more and more difficult to obtain any privacy or peace for the night anchorages.

On 1st July we entered the river Arno and ran before a kindly west wind under genoa alone, negotiating an incredible complex of 'skyhook' fishnets before eventually berthing at the Canottieri Arno in the town of Pisa. This sophisticated rowing club very kindly placed their facilities at our disposal – and how welcome were the pilfer-proof jetty, the cold showers and ice-cold drinking water!

Yes, of course we went up the leaning tower, and listened to that chap's heavenly voice echoing round the Baptistry, and sat looking at the Cathedral while drinking an extortionately expensive glass of ice-cold beer in a nearby bistro, and it was all tremendous fun.

I think on looking back at this voyage, it was our sense of complete independence and freedom which made it so memorable. We were shackled by no timetable. There were no boats nor coaches to catch nor planes with which to connect; no hotel mealtimes to interfere with one's wanderings and always there was the challenge of finding a safe berth for *Lugworm* against any inclement weather; always the possibility of returning to her and escaping to sea, or farther up a river, or into a lake. She was our constant security and, though small, supplied all our very moderate needs, for by now we were quite drunk with wandering, and used to the life aboard. We would not have changed it for the most luxurious hotel suite. Indeed, four days spent exploring Rome from the comfort of an hotel merely left us breathless and bewildered, for the tempo of that lovely city was too traumatic for a pair so completely attuned to a tranquil life.

One thing which did worry us as we entered the Ligurian Sea north of La Spezia was the alarming amount of pollution. No longer did we care to swim, for the water had turned an oily green-brown, and the ever-present litter in the sea spoke of the more industrial and tourist nature of the coast.

We had made the mistake of arranging cash withdrawal facilities at Genoa, so were forced to enter that highly industrial port. I remember on the 27th July after a torrential early morning deluge which overtook us in Santa Margherita, that the water, as we approached Genoa, was turning a sickly brown-grey. The smell of sewage was overpowering, and so unhealthy was the atmosphere that I stood out to sea again as quickly as possible having left B. to nip ashore to the bank. It was evening before we were able to escape westward and the sun had sunk when we anchored for the night just outside the charming little harbour of Arenzano.

The end of July found us in San Remo, involved in custom formalities for checking out of Italy, and in celebration of the event, we wined and dined ashore that night altogether too well. I remember down in the crowded harbour, *Lugworm* was jammed between two vast and opulent cruisers, the cigar ash from which was constantly having to be removed from her side-decks. The trouble was, her transom failed to reach the quay level by six feet or so, and on returning late that evening B. expressed some doubts as to whether she or I could manage the drop in safety.

'Nonsense, darling, I'm as sober as a Methodist,' I retorted.

'Maybe it would be best if we went for a brisk walk first,' she replied, hesitating.

'Tell you what, I'll run six times round that hut, stand on my head, then kiss you without missing,' I promised her.

I did. But I broke my toe on the hut in doing so. Still, you don't need your toes much in a boat.

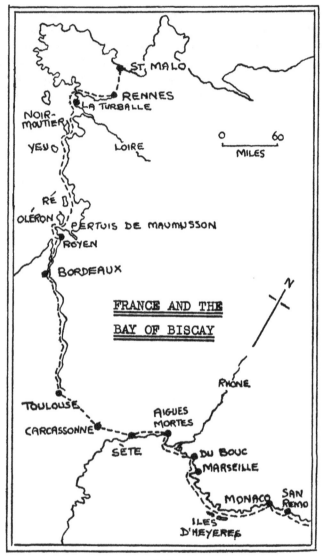

CHAPTER V

France and the Bay of Biscay

'JUST EXACTLY HOW MUCH MONEY HAVE WE?' I asked B. as we sipped our cups of coffee beneath the awning of the Cafe de Paris in Monte Carlo.

'Not nearly enough.'

I looked across the shady square where palms threw cool shadows on the grass and the gorgeous flowerbeds. The sprinklers had stopped watering the lawns, pigeons fluttered about the pavement at our feet, and the morning sun was just getting into its stride, awakening the Principality of Monaco to another uninhibited day of pleasure. 'I know,' I commented 'but in French Francs how much have we left since withdrawing the cash five days ago in Genoa?' She did a long calculation.

'Three hundred and forty-five.'

'Francs?'

'Francs. And if you're thinking what I think you're thinking, we'd better get back quickly to *Lugworm!*'

I took another pensive sip at my coffee. That was the equivalent of about £30 sterling and it had to last us until Marseille. My eyes wandered across to the imposing doors of the Casino. An important looking uniformed gentleman was fidgeting about on the elegant steps. Between the two domed towers the large windows looked dark and expensively empty.

'I won five pounds in there once long ago.'

'You were far luckier than most,' she commented. A Mercedes had drawn up at the Casino steps. The Commissionaire

163

descended to open the door, and a dark-suited gentleman emerged to ascend buoyantly and float into the foyer. The Mercedes drew silently away. I began to count the Rolls-Royces and Bentleys and other expensive cars gently circulating with the traffic past the gardens. Some of them had little flags on them and were so highly polished I could see the reflection of the palms in their bonnets. It was all very pretty. I'd counted up to fifteen before B. asked (as I knew she would), 'How did you manage it?'

'It was very cunning. I had a friend who, like you, was cautious. I was keen to go in and have a flutter and he told me I was a fool. Finally, to teach me a lesson, he bet me a fiver I couldn't come out with more cash than I went in with. I took him on.

'In those days,' I continued, 'you had to be wearing a suit to get in the place. I borrowed one of his, since the most elegant apparel I possessed at the time was flannels and a sports jacket, and armed with my fiver went into the *Salon Ordinaire*. I had only one object – to come out with more cash than I took in. I spread the whole handful of 'chips' all over the table except for three numbers, reckoning it would be exceptionally bad luck if any of those three came up. They didn't. I recovered my stake plus a winning of about sixpence. The croupier was a bit perplexed when I demanded all my chips back, but I went straight to the desk to cash them and walked out with about £5 and sixpence.'

'So you risked losing a fiver to win sixpence.'

'No, I risked losing the fiver to win five pounds and sixpence. Which I did.'

'And lost a friend instead?' she commented. I thought about that.

We paid for the coffees, and to recover idled down to the harbour where, rising like a queen above the riot of exquisite

164

luxury yachts was a magnificent white ship called 'La Belle Simone'. Her stern which was some fifteen feet away from the quay, had cleverly opened up and from it like a wasp sting projected a long elegant companionway complete with guardrails.

We watched, fascinated, as the end of the companionway hovered a few inches above the level of the quay. With each gentle surge of the sea, her stern would slowly lift and fall, and with it the companionway, but strangely its end never once actually touched the quayside. Always it hovered magically a few inches above. I drew B.'s attention to this. 'Do you know,' I pondered, 'I think it must have a photo electric cell or something hidden in the end to keep it always just that distance above the quay. Isn't it quite marvellous?' And so it was. We sat in the sun and watched the goings and comings, listening to the idle chatter aboard the boats, and slowly began to feel enormously rich. Rich.

'You know, with just a bit of luck we could recover the expenses of the whole cruise to date,' I mused. 'Just one lucky spin of the wheel up there and ...'

It was quite a thought.

We had a packet of crisps for lunch. About three o'clock we were wandering among the flowerbeds outside the Casino and finally I couldn't bear it any longer.

'Look, cuckoo, here we are actually standing outside the most famous Casino in the most famous Principality in the world, and what are we doing? Admiring the tulips! We'll never be here again, ever, you bet. Don't we owe it to ourselves just to have one little flutter ... don't we? Just for the experience? Have you ever been inside a Casino anyway? Just imagine ... with one fifty-fifty chance we could double our stake and I'll take you to the poshest restaurant in Monte Carlo this evening and we'll blue the lot on a magnificent dinner!'

That did it.

I put ten pounds in a back pocket, and she took ten pounds and I took ten pounds and in we went, all of a quiver. It was a bit awe-inspiring really: a uniformed man was approaching everyone who entered and at first we thought he was frisking them for guns, but he was only asking that cameras be left, please, at the cloakroom, no photographs inside. I don't know why, but we started talking in whispers; everybody seemed to be *sotto voce* and tense. The *Salon Ordinaire* had not altered much since I was there thirteen years before. It was just as huge and wonderfully stimulating. We had twenty quid to stake, and with one bit of luck could walk out with forty. 'If we win,' I cautioned B., 'we come out at once. No second chance to lose the lot – not us!'

I'd completely forgotten how to play and B. had never known, so between us we circulated round the tables, our pockets full of plastic 'chips' and our hearts full of hope. 'Why are some of the women wearing gloves?' came B.'s hushed whisper.

'It's to hide their fingernails, they've bitten them down to the quicks.'

'Suspense … anguish … despair. Blood.' I enlightened her and she seemed to shrink a little.

Twenty quid.

I watched a tall well-dressed aristocratic chap standing palely beside one of the tables. He was taking no part in the play, his hands thrust deep in his pockets and his eyes seemingly focused on some other world. Another man emerged from a large door which led through to the more suicidally serious gaming rooms. The newcomer looked around the tables and then, seeing the figure palely loitering, walked quickly across to him. He didn't say a word; just looked at the other fellow and there came a faint whisper in response to his silent query: 'Everything ... I've lost absolutely EVERYTHING!'

We didn't like that very much, so wandered off to another table and concentrated on the faces of the winners. There always seemed to be a winner, no matter which table we stood by; it was quite encouraging if you looked at it the right way. There was a winner every time that horrid little ball clackety-clacked into either a red or black slot on the wheel; every time the quiet voice of the croupier droned 'Faites vos jeux'.

Not once did NOBODY smile.

After about an hour of this we felt brave enough to take the plunge. I drew B. gently to one side and we sat together on an ornately upholstered settee beneath a romantic mural. I recall that in its background Diana was hunting an elk or something, and I swear she seemed to be looking at me as she drew her bow. It appeared propitious.

'Now, listen,' I cautioned B., 'It's all quite simple to understand : if we place our cash on one number only there are enormous odds against winning, but of course if we do win, we win a fortune. On the other hand if we simply place our stake on red or black-Rouge or Noir-we have a fifty-fifty chance of coming up trumps since there are only those two colours ... but only double our stake.'

I looked at her, and really, put like that it seemed quite hopeful. She thought for a while, and I could see her mind working. 'Ken,' she said. 'If that's the case, it's quite simple: put ten pounds on red and ten on black, and that way we've just GOT to win!'

It really took me aback for a minute, it seemed so simple, but after a while we got it all sorted out and she could see that it didn't work like that. 'Anyway,' I murmured, taking a deep breath, 'the great thing about this game is not to fossick about;

we'll put the whole twenty quid on one colour and take the fifty-fifty chance of doubling it, eh?' She seemed to physically shrink a bit more. Diana winked.

I took her by the hand and led her to the nearest table. 'Give me all your chips,' I hissed, sweating. I put her's and mine in a ghastly little pile, on red. 'No!' came her small voice, and I felt her hand contract in mine. 'Put it on BLACK, please put it on BLACK!'

But a man has to be decisive. Indeed, perhaps the thing I admire most about me is – I'm decisive.

Honestly, I heard that elk groan as we staggered, cold as death, out into the foyer and back into the brilliant daylight, shaking off the dark pall of that brooding malignant place.

But Oh! *Spaghetti con pommodoro*, with the occasional bag of crisps, is hard – VERY hard – to stomach in Monte Carlo; and Nice, Cannes, Raphael, St Tropez and … well, we lasted until those magnificent Îles d'Hyeres off the Cote d'Azur before decimating our dwindling traveller's cheques once again.

*   *   *

The fifth of August found us coasting close along the northern shore of the Île Levant, where clusters of fat pink nudes could be seen festooning the rocks, which wasn't surprising, this being a nudist colony. That night we fetched up in the delightful little bay of Port Man on the Île du Cros, in company with sixty-four other craft of varying size and fascination, so we were able to spend an enjoyable evening observing the aquatic habits of the Frenchman afloat.

It would seem that the average French yachting family will not consider taking to the water without the full range of pets aboard. This presents problems when it comes to the call of nature. We watched in admiration as, with sundown, dinghy

— TOILED IN ANGUISH —

after dinghy frantically rowed ashore, its feline or canine passenger straining at the bow, poised in anguish for a desperate flying leap long before the boat grounded. We found ourselves holding our breath in sympathy, exhaling with a real and shared relief as the business was satisfactorily completed. The return trip was a triumph of 'one-upmanship' as other boats in the earlier stage of the drama streaked shorewards. And do not think this drama was entirely confined to the lower species. I watched fascinated at five-thirty next morning, as head after surreptitious head peeped from cabins and then, assuming the fleet to be safely slumbering yet, a wide variety of human shapes in the altogether lowered themselves quietly over the side, floated around with an entranced expression for a minute or so, and then clambered back aboard to towel themselves in vigorous satisfaction at the success of their morning 'dip'. And what, you might ask, was I doing at five-thirty?

Well, we put into Bandol for replenishment of fuel and provisions, and at the end of that first week in August were coasting along the magnificent shore towards Cassis. Cliffs, lined with clear layers of light and dark browns, towered sheer from

169

the sea to as much as one thousand feet, and so it was one morning that we saw the awe-inspiring 'Bee de l'Aigle' rearing like a hooded predator above a thick blanket of fog, and it is a sight we shall remember for the rest of our lives. The port of Cassis was altogether too crowded for our liking so we sailed on gently westward where the cliffs became snow white, and then those incredibly beautiful 'calanques' – flooded ravines – with their wonderfully green pineclad slopes, offered shelter for a night. I remember, as we drifted silently up one of these ravines, espying an exquisite bare-breasted siren calmly planing a mast to shape in a small boatyard. Ah me ... what a WONDERFUL thing is sex.

And what hellish trouble it can cause.

But I don't recall a more inspiring sail during the whole trip than that morning *Lugworm* spanked along from those Calanques to Marseille, with the white cliffs towering a few hundred feet away and the sea so clear and deep blue that one could check by eye there was nothing for at least ten fathoms below her keel. The islands of Riou and Caleseragne, Jarros and Maire, floated like burst meringues on a sea of sapphire jelly, and Marseille – from a distance – shimmered white and unreal along the whole sweep of the Bay.

From previous experience I knew that the Rove Tunnel which used to connect Marseille with the inland lakes had collapsed years before, so we ignored the information supplied in Nice that we could enter the canal system there. We did however accept in good faith the tale at Marseille that we could enter the canals at Port de Bouc a bit farther on in the Golfe de Fos, and we entered that port hopefully on the 9th August, only to find the canal closed for reasons nobody could supply.

Nothing daunted we sailed on across the mouths of the Rhone where heaving green shallows proclaimed the strength

170

of the outflow which was meeting a slight north-running swell. We were alert at this time for the fearful 'mistral', particularly since we were finding the French forecasts impossible to translate due to their being read so very quickly. But our luck held, and after a night in the mouth of the Petit Rhone we carried light easterlies right up to Aigues Mortes, that fascinating thirteenth century fortified port from which the sea has since receded some three miles. It was here that we finally bid adieu to the Mediterranean, not without very mixed feelings, to enter the canals. *Lugworm's* mast was stowed permanently on the crutches and we began motoring along that incredible waterway system, working westward into the great Étang de Thau, a vast salt water lake north of Sète.

The transition from months of blue sea and sky, and blinding beaches, into those reedy canals with their tree-lined banks and limpid water was like a tonic. We passed into another world – the Province of Languedoc – whose marshy coastal lakes hummed each evening with a million mosquitoes and turned poor B.'s nights into a torment. Luckily, malaria has been stamped out in this area, and my own hide proved too thick – or distasteful – for the pests, but you may be sure we pressed on fast as possible. It was while trying to motor into a freshening northerly out of the port of Sete that we at last fell foul of the 'mistral' which, within half an hour, set us frantically searching for a lee, for otherwise I believe *Lugworm* might have foundered, so short and steep were the seas which were knocked up in these shallow lakes. We spent three days tucked up behind a spit sheltering from this vicious cold north wind, and used the period to collect armfuls of the rushes which line the lake banks. With these we made thick fenders, sewing them into canvas cylinders fashioned from an old boat cover we had aboard, and they protected *Lugworm's* sides from the ravages of the scores of locks we were about to pass through. We also learned the art of that very French game of 'Boule' from a strange youngster who spoke no English, but appeared to be living in a straw hut and surviving entirely on unlimited bottles of Anis, a particularly intoxicating aniseed drink. So it was not until the 19th August that we finally entered the Canal du Midi, bound for Toulouse and Bordeaux.

Life now became pastoral. The tent, when weather permitted, was unrolled each morning and stowed, but the ridgepole of our mast was left in place against sudden need to take shelter again. No night navigation is allowed on the canals, the locks being operated from seven in the morning until six each evening, and there was almost no commercial traffic and very little pleasure boating along these first southern stretches. We would motor gently on after a protracted breakfast, sometimes taking it in turns to walk along the towpath (when there was one) to stretch our legs, covering perhaps fifteen or twenty miles each day. It was very pleasant to moor up at evening and explore the small villages, taking a meal perhaps in some rustic restaurant and comparing the local wines. This region of southern France is known as the Herault and stretches roughly from Aigues Mortes along the seaboard to Valras, extending inland to north of St Christol and Lodève. The rivers Lez, Hérault and Orb form the main irrigation for the district and it grows wonderful vines. We particularly like the heady Muscat which comes from the St Jean-Minervois region.

The country here is truly beautiful. Most of the villages still have that gracious air of early French architecture in the houses and gardens, there being few recent additions by way of modern 'boxes'. We passed through thousand upon thousand of acres of vines and the occasional olive, fig and apple orchard. To my way of thinking these southern sections of the Canal du Midi are the best because, being rolling countryside, one often found one's self floating round the shoulder of hills and therefore having superb views across the adjacent valleys. As we worked north the views became more localised, and often we would have to leave the boat and climb the canal bank in order to gain some idea of the country through which we were passing. Unfortunately for us, the grapes were still not quite ready for picking.

By 24th August we were in Carcassonne, wandering round that fairytale town by day and night and marvelling at the bygone way of life it portrayed. By now we were thoroughly used to the locks, passage through which is free, and therefore placing one under obligation to take some of the burden of operation off the shoulders of their often elderly war-disabled keepers. B. would jump ashore some hundred yards before arrival and run ahead to start the procedure. If the lock was full of water – and remember that in these first stages of the system we were climbing and therefore always rising in the lock – the far gates would first have to be closed and their sluices cranked shut. Those in the near gates would then be opened to reduce the level in the lock. Once this reached the level of our section of the canal these near gates could be opened and I would take *Lugworm* in, throwing up a stern-rope first, which B. placed on the bollard, and then a headrope. It paid in such a small boat as ours to keep well back against the rear gates, so that when these were shut and their sluices closed, the onrush of water from the opening sluices at the front gates had a chance to subside a little before reaching the boat. I always kept the centreplate right up, for this underwater turbulence might otherwise have made her unmanageable in the early stages of the flooding. As the level rose, so I would take in the slack on the headrope to keep the boat against the lock side, and as soon as the level had reached that of the canal ahead, B. and the lock keeper would start to winch open the forward gates while I cast off our ropes, skimming past B.'s gate so that she could jump aboard as the boat left the lock. We carried a supply of good quality French cigarettes, handing two to the lock-keeper as we parted from each lock. Often they would be pleased to sell us eggs and fresh vegetables. B. always refused point blank to remain aboard *Lugworm*, preferring by far to help work the locks.

It was at Castelnaudary that we came across an Oceanic Catamaran, the crew of which regaled us with frightful tales of high seas between St Nazaire and Bordeaux, expressing the opinion that we were doomed if we so much as poked our nose out into the Biscay seaboard. We sat in their cabin late that night while they related accounts of mountainous swell breaking on the reefs miles offshore, and hazardous entanglements with oysterbed stakes close behind the islands; for them it was all tremendously stimulating since they had just left it all behind.

But both of us were well aware that the next leg of our voyage – up the western seaboard of the Bay of Biscay – was going to be the most dangerous phase. We had purchased a French tide table ready for calculations once we had locked out of the canals into the tidal River Garonne, and from this moment on I began thinking and living tides and Atlantic weather forecasts to get acclimatised to that great ocean once more, after two summers in the non-tidal Mediterranean. People often ask me whether we didn't get tired of the constant travelling on, day after day, with the routine of life aboard such a small boat. But to be honest, this voyage of ours brought such a rich variety of experiences that each new phase arrived before we had really got saturated with the last. The ever changing scenery, and gradually altering climate as we worked north was refreshing in itself. Add to this the constant need to assess navigational risks – and they were infinite in form, from hunches as to the effect of swell on some harbour-less coast (resulting from storms which might be ranging far away at sea), to dealing with overhead entanglements of masts in the branches of trees – all this, plus the changing language from Greek to Italian to French, and the totally different makeup of the people with whom we came into contact, formed a constant stimulation.

Once more the entire rhythm of our lives had changed. Those weeks of cat-and-mouse hopping along the desolate shores of Southern Italy already seemed a whole lifetime away. The transition from that miraculously beautiful coastline of Western Italy, south of Elba, and the excitements of the French Riviera, to this green meandering life of the inland waterways was total. Let the winds rage – what matter? The farthest we could drag would be a few hundred yards up or down the dappled canal, and suddenly from being sailors we became campers. Camping admittedly aboard a boat, but the style of life we were now living was much akin to hiking through the country, for we really did quite as much walking and exploring those charming little villages as we did boating. Moving so slowly, we had ample time to become integrated and absorb the subtly different atmospheres of the areas through which we passed. We were able to compare their individualities. Castelnaudary, Toulouse, Montbartier, Moissec, Agen and Damazan all had their own distinctive characters; I have particular reason to remember the first of September for it was that evening we moored under the towering hillside atop which perches the delightful village of Meilhan and it was here, for the first time on the voyage, I began to feel distinctly unwell.

To tell the truth, ever since our overindulgence in underwater swimming at Elba, my right ear had been giving trouble. It was a recurrence of an infection I had caught during the war, and pleasant enough at first – a mere itch which could be gratified with a stiff blade of grass or some twig of a bush inserted and twizzled about inside the ear passage, and I ask you is there anything more pleasant in life than the assuagement of an itch? This one had kept me happy for hundreds of miles. But somewhere along the line this happiness reawakened an old trouble, an infection which had laid me low thirty years before. It's not surprising really, and I got scant sympathy from B. when, during the last week in August the ear became inflamed and the inflammation spread to my neck glands, and finally my whole head became so painful that I wrapped it entire in a towel and groaned continually and things began to swell up. I couldn't move my head on my shoulders and was in frightful agony and quite ready for death.

It was (of course) B. who finally dragged me to salvation in the form of a saint – there are one or two of them about still – whose name is Docteur Girol; he lives in Meilhan, and I shall certainly send you a free copy of this book, good Docteur, for you saved my sanity if not my life – you and your young son who so patiently interpreted our troubles. Thank you, both of you, from the bottom of both our hearts, for your ministrations. Within three days, by dint of a crash course of antibiotic injections, oral ingestion and externally applied salves, the fearful malady was quite overcome; and a firm and lasting link in the *entente cordiale* of France and England was forged, especially since the good Docteur, aided by an excellent *sage femme*, refused point blank to accept any fees whatever for his services.

So, thanks to them, we were refreshed and keen to tackle the ebb and flow of the mighty Garonne when at 0800 on the 5th September we finally dropped through that enormous lock at Castets-en-Dorthe and hand in hand with the fast-flowing

176

current set off down the river under power. Five tumultuous brown swirling hours later, having somehow avoided multiple bridge supports, shoals, submerged trees and horrifyingly powerful barges, we turned to stem the current and desperately lassoo a bollard at the Sport Nautique Club just north of Bordeaux. Had the line missed, I doubt if our stouthearted outboard would have been capable of regaining the pontoon and we would have gone backwards beneath the imposing suspension bridge. But we didn't miss, and before nightfall old Lucien, custodian of the Club, had persuaded us that the safest place for *Lugworm* was resting on an antediluvian cradle drawn up on a muddy slipway clear of the frightful current and massive wakes from passing barges and ships. So we slept that night on wheels, attached to an archaic winch by a rusty steel cable, and I put chocks under those wheels just in case somebody should accidentally take off the brake.

So it was that we came to know Bordeaux, and were able to stand and gaze from the Vieux Pont, and eat exquisite things we could ill afford in some very fine restaurants; it was all totally enchanting and quite like being on holiday. Honestly – has anyone the right to enjoy life quite as much as we two?

But dammit! Isn't that what it's for?

*　　*　　*

There is no doubt whatever that the river Gironde, from its yawning mouth up to the Garonne and on to Bordeaux – some sixty miles – is tidal. We used that torrent of water sluicing out to sea to make Pauiliac before it halted in its mad onslaught, turned and rushed back up the river. On the 9th September that current again swept us relentlessly seaward until, at noon, we managed to deflect northward and hitch on to Royan, near the entrance. We made all secure in the small marina there and walked ten miles out to the Pointe de la Coubre. There we found a fine lighthouse two hundred and ten feet high which flashed its characteristic signal far across the sea to guide incoming ships into the river through a narrow channel leading between the Banc de la Mauvaise on the north side and the Battures de Cordouan southward.

It was a fresh morning, brisk with scudding clouds which rode a healthy wind from the north-west, and this added a clean scent of pinewoods to the salty tang of the sea. The birds were singing all along the lovely road that winds through the Forêt de la Palmyre. But behind their song and above the sigh of the wind there was a new and strangely disturbing background pulse – the distant mighty roar of surf. Still subdued and far off, yet it was there always in the lulls, and alien in the ears of two sailors fresh from an inland sea; yet wonderfully stimulating.

'Now,' I remember thinking to myself, 'the navigation and the seamanship begins in earnest.' In earnest it was, too. Don't imagine from this somewhat lighthearted account of our adventures that we took the business of seagoing without due care. Believe me, every heave of those equinoctial tides was calculated, every treacherous drop of a millibar noted, and so far as mortals were able to be, we were prepared for our emergence back on to the bosom of a real ocean, but even so ... even so we were still not psychologically adjusted to that traumatic switch from a blue Mediterranean to the hoary grey wastes of the Bay.

We stood at the base of the lighthouse, shielding our eyes from the spray that came driving over the dunes, and looked seaward. The sky northward was now turned a leaden grey and even the gulls, swooping above the shore, seemed to be crying a warning. Swell rolled down from the horizon to gather up, lift, and thunder down on those 'Evil Banks', and we each kept

our own thoughts as we turned inland again to continue walking northward up this fearful 'Côte Sauvage'. I was concerned
about a certain passage called the Pertuis de Maumusson five
miles up the coast which led in behind the Île d'Oleron, for
I wished to pass inland of the isle, the seaward coast of which
is rocky and ironbound, offering no succour to a small boat
which might need immediate shelter. But it is a dreadful passage according to all the pilot books and the local fisherfolk;
indeed all authorities advised strongly against its use in any circumstances. For me, however, as is the case so often at sea, it
was a matter of choosing the lesser of two evils. Despite everything, that channel was the better choice in our circumstances;
but I feared it horribly. We walked to the Pointe d'Arvert on
the south side of its entrance and sat in the marram grass on
the dunes.

It was a scene fit to turn a sailor into a stockbroker. As far as
the eye could see, heaving mountains of grey spume-wracked
ocean piled up and burst in roaring fury across the Banc des
Mattes at the opening of the channel. Over the years an exceptionally strong outflowing tide has built up a tongue of sand
and shingle off the channel's seaward end, and this reaches out
to trip up the huge Atlantic swells which roll along this coast.
In the heart of the maelstrom we could occasionally glimpse
a tiny black object: one of the channel marker buoys. So we
walked south again, turning our backs on a thin driving rain,
climbed the lighthouse and spent a fascinating hour or so chat-
ting with the keeper, of shipwreck and drowning.

But of course, we knew that all this splother and fury would
eventually die down, and I will say again that our biggest insur-
ance against disaster on this voyage was the fact that we had
time. On the 11th September we nosed cautiously from Royan
along the coast into the Bonne Anse – a shallow sandy bay un-

der the foot of the lighthouse – and our friend the keeper crossed himself on our behalf when he saw the mighty size of *Lugworm*.

The following morning, with a clear sky and a light northeast wind, we caught the tail end of the ebb to help us out to sea through the *Grande Passe de l'Ouest*, and though the fury of the wind and sea was long since spent, nevertheless poor *Lugworm* had a hard fight not to founder in the short steep overfalls. Five miles out to sea, and clear of the Banc de Mauvaise we set course north east for the Maumusson channel. It was calm, as I say, but even so there must have been a very long low oily swell still rolling in, for about a mile off the entrance to the passage there was a sickly feeling of unease about the sea, as though Neptune were sleeping very lightly and might at any moment turn over in bed, and fling us all to Hades.

We lay well off for a good hour, waiting for the tide to lift a bit and start strongly flowing in. Then, judging it safe went through hellbent under the outboard with the swirling flood behind us; it is a dreadful place for one who knows the way of the sea and swell, and it is a risk I would not lightly take again; once lucky is enough.

But now we met an unexpected hazard which besets the sailor navigating close inshore along this coast – withies. The French (like some of we English) have a weakness for shellfish. It would seem that every Frenchman within motoring distance of that shore lays claim to a patch of the seabed on which he cultivates crustaceans. This patch he marks with a multitude of tall stakes. Branches of trees, slender and bending, are thrust deep into the black ooze and there they remain, offering little resistance to wind or waves. There are forests of them as far as the horizon, and through them thread narrow straight channels which the local fishermen know well. These are quite evident if you happen to be looking straight up or down them, but once you get out of the damned channels you can freckle about for demented hours in a sort of aquatic woodland – as we did – expecting every moment to be impaled from below. I'd hate to try coping with them at night; it was bad enough in broad daylight and we had a guilty feeling as of trespassing, which seemed a bit odd at sea.

We sailed beneath the long bridge which joins Oleron to the mainland and beat up to Le Chateau on the island's eastern shore to spend a calm night in the little harbour. Next day we passed inside the Île d'Aix and made up through the narrow Rade de la Pallice between Île de Ré and the Charente region, putting into l'Aiguillon by early afternoon. It is difficult to convey the different world in which we now found ourselves. Gone was the sand and sun and baking heat, and the green and leafy waterways. Instead we were left, as the sea withdrew, to bed down on mile upon mile of black mud, and the wind – from being a welcome cooling friend – was becoming a bitter icy enemy. No doubt our blood was thinned from the months spent in the languid heat. We bought a balaclava each and an extra blanket to add to the spare sails atop our sleeping bags each night, and slowly life aboard became more difficult. It's astonishing what a difference warmth and sun can make to this primitive life we were living. Back in Greece and Italy any clothes washed in the morning were dry enough to wear by noon. But now once things got wet they remained wet for days, even after hanging in the wind. We unearthed our small gas heater and it made life more tolerable aboard in the evenings. This, with the guttering flame of two candles kept the temperature inside the tent at a bearable level and we would turn in early, listening to the flurry of wind against the canvas tent, matched by the chuckle of a fast flowing tide on the hull until, at some dark hour of the night, *Lugworm* would gently heel as she settled in the mud.

But it was still fun. In fact there was a heightened sense of adventure now we were dealing with the real sea again and we would spend hours together poring over the charts, listening to the forecasts, and absorbing all available data on the tides and currents that might be encountered on the following day's sail. Of course we worked the tides all up this coast to help make headway, and we were very lucky with the wind which remained mostly light north-easterly off the land, for which we gave thanks. By mid September we were entering Les Sables d'Olonne after a very wet cold beat against a brisk north-north-easter, glad to take shelter inside at the pontoons of the Sport Nautique north of the harbour. That night was memorable for a magnificent meal we took in *Le Dragon d'Or* restaurant which cost 80 francs and was worth every centime. Now that the weather was so much colder we were finding that we needed these hefty meals to keep up strength and morale.

The fifteen miles up the delightful coast to St Gilles-sur-Vie was completed in one day and then came another tricky stretch across the shallows inside the Île d'Yeu where the wind went foul and headed us from the north-north-west and began to freshen. It's a ghastly shore to have to leeward and I was thankful when, approaching Les Marguerites bank the wind eased. We were also now gaining protection from a long northerly swell by the bulk of Noirmoutier and those terrifying off-shore reefs which lie west of the island. In fact, in different conditions that narrow channel leading inside Noirmoutier could have been every bit as bad as the Maumusson, so we were lucky to have this fortunate protection from the swell, flying through without mishap, to once more become enmeshed in a forest of withies.

By 20th September we were in Pornic and reunited with an old friend who, it seems, had been scouring every grotto on this Biscay coast on the chance of finding us. It was a wonderful feeling, to make that very first contact with one from our own culture again, and we spent a hilarious day exploring in his car – almost forgotten luxury, a car – over the region of the Loire Inférieure. As we parted and slipped once more from the pontoon he thoughtfully threw aboard two thick horseblankets and a sou-wester.

So we worked slowly up across the mouth of the Loire, playing cat-and-mouse with the weather and finally took shelter against an unkind wind at the tiny fishing port of La Turballe. We shall remember the place, for it was here on the morning of Sunday September 24th that we happened upon a sight the like of which I doubt we'll see again.

The bay southward to le Croisic is a sweep of magnificent golden sand which flattens to run shallow out to sea in vast areas of shingle which become exposed only at very low water springs. On this day of all days – Sunday and equinoctial too – the temptation for those shellfish-orientated folk was too much. Viewed from a distance the entire bottom of the bay seemed to be crawling with black ants. We approached, and as we did so there came a sigh as of the sea stroking a shingle beach – but there was no sea. It was those thousands of humans raking the shale for cockles; but it was the manner of their raking which held us spellbound. We all know that Time and Tide wait for no man, and at most I suppose there was a short hour in which that rarely exposed seabed could be harvested. So with a concentration which was almost demented they raked, shovelled, sifted and bagged millions of flat, round, twisted and scalloped shellfish. There were Demoiselles, Coques, le Couteaux and Escargots de Mer being shovelled into plastic bags and carted with intense fury up that beach to waiting vehicles.

One and all they were far too busy to engage conversation with two ignorant foreigners, but we did spend a delirious ten minutes stalking a thighbooted hunter who was pouncing on tiny bubbles which appeared here and there, to thrust downwards deep in the sand with (you'll never believe it) a HARPOON. It was a slender steel lance with hinged barbs on the end and there, each time he withdrew it, was impinged a tubular rubber Couteau whose shell had evidently been discarded in the chase.

But WHAT in the name of baggywrinkle, I hear you groaning, has all this to do with sailing a dinghy from Greece to England? Very well; if you must have the how and the why of it all I'll give it to you. While I'm at it I might as well purge my soul and admit to an event which – quite rightly – all but put an end to our wanderings.

Anyone familiar with this coast will know that off Castelli Point just south of Piriac there is a rash of off-lying rocks and shoals extending a mile and more to seaward. It is marked by Les Bavonelles buoy. The wind was brisk from the north-north-east when we left Turballe bound for la Vilaine river and we had a splendid reach under the lee of the land with main, mizzen and genoa set. Once free of Castelli Point, however, the increase in wind decided me to hand the main. Before we had reached the Bavonelles buoy it had freshened enough to make a change to small jib advisable. I did nothing about it.

Why? Because I was getting idle and sick of changing sails and anyway we were so near to the river mouth that to hold on for another hour with that genoa couldn't matter. But the truth of the matter is I didn't want to get soaking wet, and fossicking about at the bow changing sails would mean just that.

So we cleared the point on starboard with genoa set and then I committed one of the oldest and most terrible crimes at sea. I tried to cut the corner in order to gain the lee of a headland up to windward more quickly. I TACKED INSIDE THE BUOY – for which I expect to spend a year at least in Purgatory. Within minutes I realised two things; we were in very disturbed water and we were carrying too much sail forward. I gave the helm to B. while putting myself up in the nose to change to small jib – and can you imagine anything more crassly idiotic?

The inevitable happened. We were beating over shoals which humped the seas into short steep chops and with my weight forward poor *Lugworm* just couldn't rise quick enough. I heard B.'s startled warning, looked up and got a hogshead of solid water in the chest which swept me aft of the cockpit and knocked some sense back into my addled head. For a moment it was all Hell with both of us bucketing the sea back where it belonged and *Lugworm* staggering manfully, her cockpit awash. I hardened the mizzen and she kept her nose into seas and looked after us while we drifted stern-first out of that shoal into safe deep water, praying meantime that nothing more would come aboard, nor up through the bottom as we did so. And why do I tell you all this? Because maybe I can brush off just a bit of that salutary lesson which nearly stopped the hearts of myself and my crew – namely NEVER to get careless and take the sea for granted.

We bailed her back to safety but I can tell you it was touch and go for a while. And then we rounded Castelli again with mizzen and small jib set, OUTSIDE the buoy this time, to have a hard wet fight up to the Vilaine river. We were thankful to get in.

* * *

One day when we are senile as well as old the two of us are going to get on our bicycles and pedal off to Plymouth where we shall board the Roscoff Ferry and set off to potter in the peninsula of Brittany. We made this vow during the next ten days of our voyage through those delightful canals, for we quite fell in love with the area. There is something subtly different about them for they are narrower and more overgrown; more like our own small inland rivers as they meander quietly along, and there is also a great affinity between the Breton people and the Cornish folk from back home. The Vilaine river, which until recently used to flow into the sea just north of the Loire, has now been dammed at Arsal about five miles up from the mouth. The lock there is huge, but once through it one moves into a different world where the river winds through a wide flat valley between reedy banks, and fat cows graze in green meadows. There were few vines here, the cultivated land being used mainly for growing maize. Roche Bernard, a sleepy little village with a small inlet where floating pontoons are available for berthing, is a good point from which to explore the area and it was there, after a superb meal in the auberge *Les Deux Magots*, that we took our first hot bath since the disaster at the Torre dell'Ovo in the Gulf of Taranto five months before.

The next four days were spent idling through Redon, Besle, Messac and Molière and on Friday 29th September we passed through Rennes. I would strongly advise any voyager to avoid its waters if possible, so polluted are they from the industrial city. On the last day of September in the early dusk we made fast to the left bank just beyond the St Germaine lock and wandered up a hill to the small village in search of a meal. The place seemed asleep and no sign of any restaurant was to be found, but a matronly lady from whom we made enquiries assured us this was not the case. 'Est ce que vous avez visité la Crêperie de Madame Lecoq Oubret?' she enquired. We assured her we had not and forthwith she gave us directions, asking that we please inform the good Madame Lecoq that it was she who directed us there, and none other, much less chance fortune.

We followed her advice and soon stood before a large establishment combining, it seemed, a crêperie, restaurant and shop. But alas, it was securely locked. Inside, however, there was movement, and without seeming too inquisitive we could make out the figure of Madame amid a display of confections. She was ironing a pair of trousers – and looking occasionally at us. Still loath to give up hope we remained, examining the contents of the window and before long saw her spit on the base of the iron, survey it for a moment, then place it carefully on a folded cloth at the end of the table. With that she came to the door opened it a fraction and raised her eyebrows.

'Madame,' we explained, in doubtful French. 'Nous sommes voyageurs avec un bon appetit. Mais calamité! Ici dans St Germaine c'est evident qu'il n'est pas possible à manger. Et vous, recommendé par la bonne Madame ... êtes aussi fermé!'

At this the good Madame, who must have been approaching 70, cocked her head sideways, looked us up and down, and then in a surprisingly resonant and manly voice which seemed to be operating under great pressure exclaimed in French that indeed she was shut, and the season being over she feared there was nothing in the house; and she took another look at us; but wait a minute; she would have words with Pierre, for after all perhaps she could knock up a little something if we did not mind sitting among the groceries and keeping an eye on the iron while she looked into the matter?

After a while she returned with the news that if we were prepared to accept such miserable fare she might manage perhaps a little melon with port to start with followed by homemade paté, hamburgers in savoury rice, washed down with a bottle of Chambertin (rouge). To end the meal, alas there was only chocolate caramel, cheese, coffee and grapes.

We did in fact manage to accept this offering and before long, Pierre himself came to examine these odd late foreigners. Soon, the three of us were engaged in animated conversation, round the board table while Madame continued with the ironing of Pierre's trousers. By now it was known that I was an ex-Service man. Of the Navy, it was true, and therefore not perhaps directly connected with the land fighting which had raged in the area towards the end of the war. But as soon as he knew that my elder brother had lost his life in one of the assaults south of Caen, we were like blood brothers, Pierre and I. Ancient war maps showing the invasion beaches and the main assault routes were soon laid over an adjacent table which was drawn up to ours, and between the paté and the cheese I learned more of the strategy involved during those perilous months than any history book will ever supply, in-terspersed with a recipe for apple pie from Madame, the whole lingered over with a second bottle of the excellent Chambertin.

But it's strange, isn't it, how the little things stick in the memory; like lingering down on the canal bank in the night after we had parted from this very lovable couple, watching the swarm of furry moths on the bridge above battering their brains out against the glass of the glowing lamp.

Just because it – and they – were there.

*   *   *

It was on the morning of Monday the 2nd October, lying alongside the quay at St Domineuc which is close to that delightful little town of Dinan, that a sort of depression set in.

Of morale, that is. The night had been one of torrential rain and everything in the boat felt damp including our sleeping bags. Came the dawn with a continuing fine drizzle percolating through a grey morning mist, and suddenly all the horror of returning to our indescribable climate; the coming winter and the undealt-with Tax Returns and accumulated overdue National Health Stamps – the whole lot loomed like a desolate dreary battle field ahead, and suddenly it seemed a hell of a long way from Corfu. Add to this the fact that I'd upset a full carton of milk on the after deck while brewing up the morning cup of tea, most of which had gone down my neck and into my sleeping bag. Things, one way and another, were in a bit of a mess and dammit there are times when you can be joyous and times when you can't.

At such moments it's not a bad policy to deliberately set about boosting one's ego. 'Cuckoo,' I addressed the nose on the far side of the centreplate casing, 'don't you think I'm ...'

Wait a minute, I'll start again.

'Cuckoo, don't you think we are brave?'

There was a long pause while one eye extricated itself from folds of bedding, opened, swivelled about and then focused on me.

'Brave,' I repeated. 'Don't you think we're very brave and ought to be famous? Dammit we've voyaged over three thousand miles in *Lugworm* since we left Fowey last year. Don't you think when people hear all about it they'll think we're brave; I mean, in a way aren't we in the same bracket as Cabot and Raleigh and Vasco da Lopez; just on a smaller scale?'

The eye continued looking at me. The rain began beating down another tattoo on the tent above. 'Think of all the perils we've survived. Shipwreck, strandings, sunstroke ...' I couldn't think of any more and anyway the wooden rib halfway down

Lugworm's cockpit was cutting a slot into my starboard liver and it hurt. I turned over and drew up one knee (it was just possible to do this without widening *Lugworm* amidships). The bruise on the other hip started boring a hole into the bottom boards. Long ago had we given up the useless task of inflating our airbeds; they were flat again within minutes, in fact the whole of the Riviera had been a succession of breathless nights.

'Courageous,' I said. 'Empire Builders!'

'I think I am,' she said.

Suddenly the sleeping bag felt damper and the Tax Returns much worse.

'You're a sailor, born and bred,' she went on (which wasn't true anyway), I never profess to be one. For me the sea is a vast unknown peril; it's ME that's the truly courageous one. Real courage is doing a thing even though you're scared stiff; yes, I think I AM brave.'

I thought about that. 'OK' I came back fighting, 'So I'm a seasoned salt and the sea holds no terrors (Oh, Ha Ha!) for me, but I'm courageous in other ways surely? Remember when that festoon in the thirty-knot gin palace rocked the boat off Cannes and a litre of boiling water went all over my foot? Did I shriek? No: I simply dunked my foot over the side.'

'And I did everything else for the next fortnight,' she chipped in.

Things were bad. It wasn't going the way I'd planned, this dialogue, at all. It was bad enough to be wet and miserable, but to be wet and miserable and unappreciated was intolerable. I told her so.

'It isn't that you're unappreciated, it's just that you're quite intolerable when you're wet and miserable,' she retorted. Hell, things were getting worse.

190

'When we get ashore I'm going to tell somebody all about what we've done,' I mumbled. 'I'm going to see the local newspaper proprietor and sell our story to the highest bidder.'

'In St Domineuc?'

'When we get to Dinan, then.'

'In French? That should make good reading.'

You can't win.

IT WASN'T ALL JOY

We went ashore, moist and hungry to search out the local breadshop. They had no bread. The village was a long straggle of depressing houses either side of a busy straight road that came from somewhere and went, I suppose, to somewhere else; it didn't seem to matter much where. We walked about a bit and bought an umbrella which was slightly damaged.

191

No; it wasn't ALL joy.

But spirits tend to rise with the barometer, and by the following morning, when we dropped down into the tidal River Rance through another huge lock, L'Écluse de Chateliers, we both felt better, and even a bit dry, which was a good thing for it was low water in the river with oceans of thick black mud everywhere which wasn't uplifting. By midday, after picking our way carefully downstream we were approaching the colossal hydro-electric barrage which uses the rise and fall of the sea to generate a great deal of electricity, and we felt rather like a flea in a coffin as the gate clanged shut on us in that gigantic lock and the water level began to fall; and when the other gates opened, there again were the hoary grey wastes of the Atlantic. By early evening we were locking into the basin at St Malo and – Hah! – Fame at Last – a reporter with a camera made us turn round and come in again to look as if we'd just arrived, and our photograph (looking as if we'd just arrived) was in the next edition of the *Ouest France* with a remarkable and slightly accurate news item beneath.

'I look a bit thin,' I said to B., thumbing the photo over a coffee in the old town.

'My hair looks as if it could do with a good wash,' she replied. 'Do you think ...'

'Mon Dieu!' came the exclamation from alongside. A wild looking figure in a mackintosh was reading the same paper. 'C'est vous!' he added, looking from the paper to us and back again. 'Merveilleux! But in such a little boat ... and to take so long ... you must be very rich!'

'I am,' I replied as we pooled our last centimes for the coffee. 'Immensely. In fact I have shares in a goldmine!'

And I took her hand as we walked out.

CHAPTER VI

The Final Stretch

IF YOU LOOK AT THE CHART of the approaches to the English
Channel you will see that in distance there is really not much
to choose between Guernsey to Start Point or Cherbourg to
Portland Bill.

We had been weighing up this problem while pottering
through the canals, and at first we were inclined towards going up through the Channel Islands, then shooting across direct from Guernsey to Start Point. But we had spent too long
eating, enjoying ourselves and being ill and the weather had
turned unsettled. Mists, sea-fog and autumn squalls were
not uncommon, and I knew the power of the tides and swell
between those rocky off-lying reefs and islands, so finally we
thought it safer to stick close to the coast of the mainland, work
up round Cap de la Hague, and then strike north from Cherbourg.

Another alternative, of course, would have been to work
eastward along the north coast of France until the Channel
narrowed at Boulogne, then nip across to Newhaven, but this
would have involved more than two hundred and fifty more
miles before we had clawed back westward again to Portland,
and now, for the first time on the cruise, we were becoming
concerned with the lateness of the season.

The early morning forecast on 5th October (we were now
picking up the BBC transmissions) gave a probable easterly
force six to seven, which is no good in a dinghy, so we spent the

day exploring St Malo, cashing traveller's cheques and buying a series of large scale Blondel's French coloured charts of this coastline.

I quote from my log for the following day, to indicate how the hour by hour details of the trip were recorded -without which it would have been impossible to write this book.

Friday 6th October 1972
Barometer: 1002 Rising slightly.
Forecast: Easterly force 5-6 becoming south-east.
0630 De-rigged tent and rigged boat for sea. Approached lock entrance but had to await the 0800 opening. 0800 Locked into exit. Bright clear sunny morning with light S.E. wind. Tide flowing west approx. one knot.

0900 Off the Petit Bey island set course under all sail 050 Compass for Pointe de la Varde. Wind light E.S.E. 1015 Anchored in entrance to Rotheneuf Bay to await easing of adverse tidal stream which was now running westerly approx. one to two knots. Wind remaining light E.S.E.

1130 Weighed and proceeded under power, wind very light easterly.

1245 Anchored in Anse du Verger and went winkling on the rocks for lunch.

1445 Tide now slack, wind very light easterly. Weighed and motored toward La Fille buoy off Pointe du Grouin.

1520 Off La Fille Buoy. Tide setting 115 degrees True at 2¾ knots. Set compass course 030 for Granville (allowing 35 degrees offset for strong tide to make good 065 degrees) and using transit of the Herpin Lighthouse and the Pointe du Grouin to check trackline. Visibility a bit misty, but allowance for drift seems about OK. This inset to the Baie du Mont St Michel is tricky.

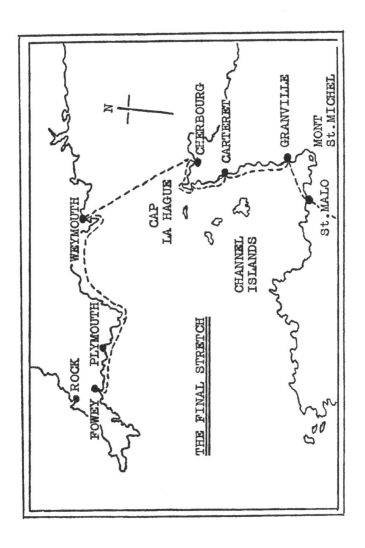

THE FINAL STRETCH

1600 Sighted faint white houses above horizon. Granville. Wind fallen to nil.

1700 Wind coming in very light north east.

1715 Came to buoy inside harbour to await lock. Many fishing boats also waiting.

1745 Entered inner basin and berthed at very crowded marina. Shopped for fillets of fish and supped aboard with fish and white sauce and sweet wine, mashed potatoes and fresh watercress.

The notes for that day, which I always kept on the right hand pages of the log read as follows:

The strong tide (approaching three knots) ran 115 degrees True off the Herpin Light then swung to 090 True about three quarter way across the Bay. A marked overfall was visible all along the shallow bank off the shore. Gannets and shearwaters are here in abundance, also shoals of tiny fish which dive on our approach giving the appearance of raindrops in the water. Sky is absolutely free of cloud but visibility a bit misty. Wind disappointing, but came in from north east about two miles off Granville.

Granville is a flourishing fishing port with inner dock basin (single gate only) in front of a busy shopping centre. Behind this, and climbing up the hillside is the old fortified town the western end of which appears to be a military barracks. We closed Le Loup tower off the entrance, leaving it to starboard and entered the outer harbour which is surrounded entirely by quays, and as soon as the influx of fishing craft were through we followed them in and berthed at the very crowded marina. We are the fifth boat out! A notice on the Yacht Club door states that due to overcrowding visiting yachts cannot be welcomed by the Club after the 27th August. However, we do not consider ourselves a yacht, and nobody has come to molest us, yet.

We had now completed two thousand two hundred and thirty-six miles by my reckoning since we left Kassiopi, and the crew was, to put it mildly, becoming somewhat weathered. Foogoo, from being stained a hideous green of the African jungles, had taken on a sort of grained soapstone colour, with veins of brown showing through where intense heat had cracked the wood. He remained, however, as belligerently in charge and competent as ever. We other two members having passed through that mahogany-bronze stage of sunburn, were now turning an Oriental yellow; the sort of deep sallow colour of boiled leather soaked in curry powder, and reminiscent of retired Indian Army Colonels. The health of all aboard was, however, unchanged, and I really think we were both as wiry as two centipedes.

The following morning, 7th October, we left Granville at 0700 and sailed before a light south-easterly up towards Carteret, carrying the ebb stream up the coast until about 1345 when we had to motor against an hour of adverse flood, the wind having once more deserted us. By 1445, after a run of 34 miles, we were anchored off the entrance which has a long stone breakwater jutting out from magnificent sand dunes with the shallow entry channel on its eastern side. The sand dunes to the west soon give way to rocky cliffs off Cape Carteret. The entrance channel is long and bottomed with shingle, swinging to the east as it goes in, and the flood stream scoured in like a mill race. Inside, and past the little town which lies all on the north bank, it opens into a huge shallow marsh, somewhat muddy and grassy. We found the town unprepossessing, being mostly modern houses with no character, but the environs might well be worth exploring more fully.

The next day was hilarious. The wind remained nonexistent, for which, frankly at this point I was thankful, for the chart in vivid red lettering off the Cap de la Hague, has the warning 'VERY VIOLENT CURRENTS, DANGEROUS BREAK-ERS WHEN WIND IS CONTRARY TO TIDAL STREAM', and as it turned out had there been a fair breeze from the south (which would have been the one we wanted) it might have been a tricky rounding. I have to admit to a complete navigational bish-up here for which I've still not found the cause. My tidal stream calculations for 8th October 1972 taken from the inset tidal stream atlas on Blondel's chart gave me to think that at midday we would have a comfortable north-east running stream of about one knot to help gently ease us round this dangerous Cape. On arrival, however, it soon became evident that abeam of La Foraine beacon, with the outboard running at full revs and little help from the wind, we were making half a knot backwards. The tide had thrown Blondel's predictions overboard and we spent a frigid half hour homing-in on a bearing of 040 degrees for the light-house which took us clear of the appalling off-lying rocks until we were free of the main strength of the tide. Thereafter we were able to nose gingerly into a tiny little crack in the reefs called Goury where *Lugworm* was carefully positioned to dry out on just about the only few feet of flat bottom to be found. The scene at low tide looked rather like a Martian landscape, so prolific were the fangs of barnacle encrusted rock all around.

It was evident that we were not going to round that Cape until the tidal stream turned, and in some perplexity I made enquiries at a row of coastguard cottages close ashore, to receive totally wrong information once again, which finally led to our motoring in a flat calm round that cape against a three knot adverse flow. Our experience was that the stream regardless of flood or ebb ran in a south-westerly direction close under the light. Maybe it was a local back-eddy, but certainly to the north of the light it remained running in a westerly direction all the rest of that afternoon, and in desperation we motored into St Martin's Bay having failed to find a berth in Port Racine, which must be the smallest harbour in Europe; the berthing warps of the few fishing boats therein quite precluded even *Lugworm* finding a niche.

That night was spent uneasily off an exposed beach – a thing I never relish – but the following morning with a brisk southerly we hoisted all sail and set off for the Bréfort Buoy. Once more, however, the stream predictions on Blondels proved quite wrong and we met an adverse flow of great force which was knocking up a nasty sea with an easterly swell on top of it all. So we tried again that evening and succeeded in rounding Bréfort buoy and making a bit of southing past La Coque and Le Hoquet rocks to round l'Etonnard Beacon and enter Omonville harbour very wet and thoroughly chilled through.

You will have gathered that the tides in this tricky area were determined to beat us, but we were more determined that they should not. On Tuesday 10th October, we closed a local fishing boat just off Omonville entrance and enquired when, if ever, the stream ran towards the east. 'But immediately after low water!' came the surprised reply, 'When else?' So it may be, but it certainly did not run eastward close inshore where we were and once again, with a forecast of freshening north-easters we battled against an adverse three knot tide with sails and engine giving everything they could for I was keen to enter Cherbourg before the arrival of a predicted 'low' which might pin us up a beach somewhere on an exposed bit of the coast. At 1700, after a hard fight we gained the lee of the Grande Rade breakwater of that superb harbour.

The yacht club proved shut for the 'vacances annuelles' from 2nd to 16th October, but we learnt at a temporary office, that our stay at the pontoons would cost six francs a day which was reasonable enough, even though there were no toilet or shower facilities. So we went ashore and ate at the Cafe Theatre: Moules Marinière and Côte du Pore followed by cheese and caramel pudding with a bottle of reasonable red wine and it cost us forty francs which, at eleven francs to the pound was a bit shattering, but worth it.

Yes, it was a triumph, but oddly disturbing, to arrive at Cherbourg. It meant the end of our foreign travelling and in a way was a climax to our adventures and yet, when we thought about it, the 'hop' that now faced us was a greater challenge than anything which had gone before. Seventy-five miles as the crow flies north to Weymouth may not sound much, but for *Lugworm* it represented some eighteen hours sailing across open water and directly across all the major traffic lanes.

Torrential rain beat down all that first night and by morning the winds had swung northerly and were beginning to knock up a nasty grey sea over there towards England. We explored the town and earmarked the likely cheaper backstreet restaurants for evening meals ashore, spending a small fortune in the 'launderette' getting our wet and dirty gear cleaned and dried. Thursday 12th October saw that particular 'front' pass over with the usual gusty clear skies following on, and a forecast of force four to five north-easterlies which was little use to us. Our plan was to await a southerly slant and fair forecast, but we took this opportunity to lighten *Lugworm* for the crossing by off-loading a heavy bag full of unwanted gear such as clothing, snorkelling equipment, books, charts, and this type-writer, to a friend in a large yacht with whom we arranged a rendezvous at his home in England. It was wise to bring *Lugworm*'s freeboard up a bit if we could, and I looked to the watertightness of her hatches, checked the rocket flares and daylight distress signals and generally reviewed all the safety measures, working backwards from the ultimate disaster of a complete swamping, or being run-down. Over and over again in our minds we went through the exact action to be taken in the event of emergency.

Meanwhile the wind increased from the north. Yachts came running in with blown-out sails, their crews red-rimmed about the eyes, and salt grimed. They would surge down under head-sails through that narrow channel from the Petite Rade and make fast quickly to any empty slot on the pontoons. For the next four hours or so they would die, and reports came in of leaving England with fair following winds only to encounter ever freshening conditions as they made more southing, un-til the last twenty miles or so proved a bit of a pounder, with splendid seas running. We stood on the weather end of the quays and watched as ever increasing swells rolled down and burst over the top of the breakwater to weather of the Grande Rade, and wondered if, after all, we were not biting off a bit more than we could chew.

All Friday and Saturday the wind remained force five to sev-en from the north-east and the seas steadily built up while the temperature dropped. We always seemed to be cold, slightly moist, and found it hard to keep up morale, now that we were so near home and yet still so far away. All that Cherbourg had to offer was sampled, and then we took to making sorties far-ther afield along the rather distressing suburbs but it was all rather lacking in uplift. The *Patisserie Paris* on the corner of the Place de Gaulle was a constant but expensive relief from approaching boredom, and the *Prisunic* supermarket claimed much of our time wandering around the counters; at least it was warm and dry, which is more than could be said for *Lugworm*, bless her. Our berthing warps were becoming very oily and somebody burned a hole in the tent by dropping a cigarette thereon. Things were a bit depressing, and still the wind kept up its constant howl from the north. Forecasts of gale force nine in the adjacent areas kept us pinned to that pontoon and by 13th October we were so bored that we began to think terrible thoughts of shipping *Lugworm* across on the ferry steamer.

'It's not a bit of use risking our necks just for the vanity of saying we sailed right home,' I remarked to B. one horrible wet evening as we sheltered in the port harbourmaster's office watching the rain and fast scudding clouds. 'This is just the sort of situation that leads to disaster, going against one's better judgement simply to "pull it off".'

I looked through the gathering dusk to the ferry terminal. Above the sheds we could see a funnel rearing; evidently the Townsend-Thoresen ferry was berthed. It would do no harm just to wander over and make a few enquiries. The wind was soughing through those huge deserted sheds, banging the doors and rattling windows, and the squalls of sleety rain pattered in grey sheets along the empty quays. We hugged one wall for shelter and B. looked up at the ferry's sides, towering above us. 'I'd no idea,' she remarked, 'they were quite so big!'

'It's just the contrast after *Lugworm*,' I told her. 'They're tiny, as ships go, but they're a damned sight bigger than we have been used to for the last eighteen months.' As we idled along the quay we could hear the deep humming of her generator from somewhere within.

Then I felt B. catch my arm. She had stopped, and was pointing upward. 'Er ... darling,' she said. 'Look!'

It was *Queen Elizabeth II.*

*   *   *

By 22nd October we were both thoroughly fed up with Cherbourg, and despairing of the weather. But finally the wind swung out of the north-east and settled in the west though it kept up its strength of around force five, and the seas kept rolling in. 'But it just MUST ease off soon!' B. kept saying, as we trailed in and out of the very excellent and helpful Harbourmaster's office where a daily weather chart was posted. And of course it did. It happened very suddenly and really caught us a bit unawares. We'd just completed a long and enjoyable evening meal of shellfish in our favourite lowdown 'dive' and when we came out into the street in the darkness a strange feeling came over us; something was missing. The howl of the wind had ceased. We both looked up to where, palely through a layer of mackerel clouds the moon was glowing. We just looked at each other and started running, calling in for a quick last minute check in the Pilot's Office where a kind official telephoned the local Met. station and confirmed that for the next twenty-four hours nothing violent was on the books. In fact the immediate forecast for the night was calm variable winds.

We raced back to *Lugworm*, dropped 100 francs into the Clubhouse box for outstanding dues, and got the boat ready for sea. She was fully fuelled, and within twenty minutes we were coiling down the tarry warps and nosing northward into the Grande Rade. It was 2300 as we cleared the end of the outer mole, and started dancing in the seas which were still running from the recent winds. With all sails set we steadied before

203

a light southerly breeze on a course of 338 by compass, and the lights of Cherbourg winked 'goodbye' astern.

Oh, but it was an exciting moment, that parting from France. If fate willed, we would be hearing English spoken again all around us by the following night, and really be home! It was hard to believe. As the Cherbourg lights grew dim astern we picked up the farewell flash of Cap de la Hague and then it was just a case of praying that the winds would stay in a southerly sector and behave themselves for a while. I knew that, striking across the tidal streams as we were, we would be carried first one way and then back again, and my calculations indicated that the ebb would just about cancel out the flood. We took it in turns sleeping for an hour at a time and keeping a good watch for the constant traffic up and down the Channel. Like necklaces of lights the ships crossed ahead and astern, but only twice was there danger of collision or swamping from too-close approach to the huge wakes of tankers – and then the risk was easily avoided. I feared that our tiny navigation lights might be missed, and frankly the radar reflector clanging up there on the starboard shroud was more for morale than anything else. I think on that crossing *Lugworm* really felt smaller than at any other time on the cruise; maybe it was just that we were again sailing in home waters and the true perspective of what we were doing and had already done suddenly came home to us.

The wind remained kind, light from the south-west, and we helped it out a bit at times with the engine. There was just a small and violent whirlwind which funnelled the clouds down to meet the sea at dawn on 26th October as we peered ahead, keen for the first sight of England; and at 0810 we sighted Portland Bill fine on the starboard bow.

Crumbs ... but it seemed incredible. How many lights had we sighted, how many headlands had we approached, how of-

ten had we watched as the land beyond slowly materialised …
again and again over the last seven months of the voyage home?
But not one of them looked like this.

We just keep looking, and slowly the land became clearer,
and we could actually see the Dorset hills. Then, for us, a very
splendid thing happened. Out of the north the long lean grey
shape of a warship came speeding down. With a white bone
in her teeth Her Majesty's Frigate 190 hove up at full speed,
circled us, and sped off again on her business. It was like a
welcoming handshake reaching out even before we had made
port, though I suppose they were really just wondering what
the Hell we were doing out there in something that looked like
the Captain's gig.

Feeling rather self-conscious I tied the yellow 'pratique' flag
to the shroud as we nosed into Weymouth at 1500 and the
Customs Officer was on station ready and waiting at the base
of the quay steps. No sooner were we moored safely up in the
harbour than the television crew and reporters hove-up and we
had to leave again and sail back, looking as if we had just arrived. It was all very exciting really, watching it on colour TV
that night in the local pub, and we kept saying to each other at
odd moments 'Hush … remember these people can tell what
we're talking about!' And 'We've done it – we've really done it,
haven't we? Doesn't it feel a bit queer?'

So we booked in at the local concert hall and basked in the
music of the Bournemouth Symphony Orchestra, and late that
night ate fish and chips sitting on a bench on Weymouth Prom
… and felt dreadfully English, and glad of it, arrogant beggars
that we are.

On the 8th of November, drenched with sea-fog we entered
Fowey harbour and grounded gently on the beach up Mixtow
Creek. The round trip was completed, and suddenly there

were Brian and Shirley – those two stalwarts who had towed us overland from this port more than two thousand miles to Volos in Greece. It seemed an incredibly long way back to that dusty hot morning when they had waved goodbye just south of Mount Olympus.

But, for me, the oddest thing was – there was finally nowhere else to go. I looked around for a bit, feeling strangely unsettled, and then I kissed B. very long and hard, for it seemed as good a thing to do as anything.

And really, I think she deserved it, don't you?

Thoughts

IT WASN'T A 'DO OR DIE' VENTURE THIS, though it had its moments, and really I know we were very lucky to get *Lugworm* back more or less intact. A thousand ill chances might have resulted in complete disaster.

People often ask us what, if anything, we might alter in the planning should we with hindsight do the same voyage again. It is a difficult question to answer for it all depends on what one is seeking from such a venture. For instance, we now know that from the purely sailing point of view it would have been better to do the whole thing the other way round and sail from England to Greece. That way we would have been able to use the light north-westerlies right down the coast of Italy, and no doubt the time taken would have been shortened. But from our point of view that would have been a sad loss, for it was just the fact that often we could not gain ground northward that kept us pinned for days at a time in many really fascinating out-of-the-way harbours.

Again, people have commented that it was odd to arrange our arrival in Greece just as the fearsome northerly 'meltemi' was getting into its stride for the summer. But again I reply that dealing with that wind was, surely, half the challenge of that fantastic summer in 1971 when we were playing cat-and-mouse with the elements around the Aegean. Had it not been for that wind we might never have spent the incredible month in Santorini living in a pumice cave, or known the sheer elemental roar of a near hurricane for four days on a beach under Andros Isle; and such memories are worth more than money and will be with us all our lives.

Would we, with hindsight, have chosen a different boat? Bigger perhaps, with a cabin? The answer is no. *Lugworm* fulfils all that we needed on this voyage. A larger boat, while providing more comfort, would have denied us entry to all those rivers, and innumerable scrambles up beaches. Believe me there is a tremendous sense of satisfaction to be got from sitting in your boat at the top of a shingly beach listening to the thunder of the waves a few feet away – knowing that, no matter what the wind and the sea care to brew up you're out of their reach. You can't do that in a larger boat; you're just kept desperately buzzing about looking for harbours and often, on a trip like this, there aren't any. Who wants harbours anyway?

Of course on such a venture you have to be fit. Really fit – and we both were. But after all, if you're going to enjoy life haven't you got to be fit anyway? One couldn't enjoy this sort of trip nearly as much unless the sheer joy of using one's muscles hard, and then completely relaxing afterwards, was a normal routine. I think the constant hard physical work would soon exhaust a slack person. Being small helps too.

Experience? Of course thirty years spent handling small boats in all conditions breeds a margin of safety through sheer instinct, and this undoubtedly stood us in good stead and it's something which cannot be acquired otherwise. But I would say that a less experienced person planning the same sort of venture would run little greater risk of disaster provided he was not a fool. And that means simply taking a sensible stock of the situation each day before sailing, carefully weighing up the risks, and then not being ashamed of deciding to stay ashore, even when the decision proved groundless. That's good seamanship; it gets you home.

There is nothing by way of equipment we would have changed; our two-burner meths stove worked excellently, and you really can't beat candles for lighting – they're waterproof and non-rusting and will light when taken straight from waterlogged bilges. Two anchors and plenty of warp are essential, and though we never set them the spare suit of sails kept us warm on many occasions.

As for the engine; well, four horsepower is little enough, but again doesn't this make for a greater challenge? After all, if you can simply turn a switch and speed at fifteen knots to the nearest port – well, that's motor boating. The great thing is reliability; you've got to KNOW it's going to work every time you need it, and our Mercury did this without fail, omitting the time I filled the coil with salt water which is a bit unfair. You have to weigh up the fuel situation too; our seven gallons was good for seventy miles or so pottering along at four knots. No; I'd have the same engine if doing it all again.

One thing I would strongly advise, and that is to make sensible provision for cash withdrawals at selected points before leaving England. We did this through Lloyds and the machinery worked very smoothly. To be able to go into some unpronounceable place at the back end of beyond and calmly cash a cheque is very satisfying, and it was only when the Pound Sterling was 'floated' halfway up Italy that we were ever denied this facility – and then only for two days. But of course you've got to have the cash and this entire trip cost us about £1,600 excluding the cost of the boat and engine. It could have cost us a lot less of course but we spent more and more cash on meals ashore as the weather got colder in France – and that's expensive. One can argue that it would probably have cost that living at home anyway over a period of eighteen months; and we were fortunate enough to rent our house for the entire time which paid the rates.

Finally, the crew. Complete compatability is essential if one is going to get the most from such a jaunt. It is more important than natural aptitude, provided the skipper knows what he's doing. B. is, frankly, not a sailor, the sea for her is an alien thing and she is not really at home on it, which speaks volumes for her very real courage in tackling this voyage.

I would not have done it without her.

So together we did it, and now *Lugworm* is upside-down on the lawn behind the house and Foogoo glowers from the mantelpiece. Just occasionally we find ourselves out there looking at her scars; and suddenly one of us will say: 'Do you remember where that happened! What was the name of that idiot who ...' And off we go into dreamland.

It's fun!

Lugworm

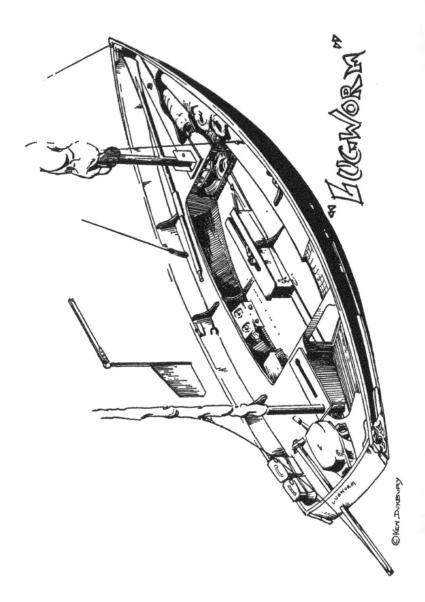

"LUGWORM"

© Ken Duxbury

LUGWORM

Lugworm is a Drascombe Lugger
designed by John Watkinson,
and was built by Doug Elliott

Length: 18ft
Beam: 6ft 3in
Draught (plate up):   10in
(plate down):   3ft 6in
Total weight (approx):   1,000 lb
Total sail area: 130 sq ft
Rig: Gunter Yawl
Outboard: Mercury longshaft 4hp
Centreplate: Half-inch steel, 120 lb
Rudder: Quarter-inch steel, 29 lb
Construction: Thames Marine plywood